FROM SEA TO SHINING SEA:
More Soldiers' Angels Recipes from the 50 Glorious States

FOREWORD

Many special thanks are extended to the following Angels who have made this cook book possible: Angel Angel Thompson for the idea of collecting recipes from every state to enhance a postcard book for one of her Officials; Angel Sharon Moody for suggesting that another cookbook was needed; Angel Deanna Heitschmidt for the cover artwork; Angel Pat Miller for diligently seeking out recipes from friends and family and spreading the news about Soldiers' Angels; Angel MaryAnn Foote for overseeing the project; everyone who contributed their recipes and photos; and any and all Angels who assisted in making this book a reality.

Angel Hugs,

Jeff Bader
Co-founder
March 3, 2009

INTRODUCTION

How better to celebrate the bounty that is America's than with a cookbook! *From Sea to Shining Sea: More Soldiers' Angels Recipes from the 50 Glorious States* does just that. All 50 states are represented with recipes that highlight locally grown foods, local customs, or local heritages. Many of the recipes are time-honored, traditional recipes that Grandma or Great Grandma dished up with love to her family during WWII, the Korean War, or even the Vietnam War. Other recipes, also prepared with love, reflect current trends in eating and cooking. Even if you do not consider yourself a cook or a baker, you will find *From Sea to Shining Sea* a delightful read.

This book is the third in the series of cookbooks published by Soldiers' Angels. The first book was *Angel Delights: Treasured Cookie Recipes from Soldiers' Angels and Friends.* The second cookbook was *Cooking with Angels: May No Soldier Go Unloved or Unfed. Treasured Recipes from Soldiers' Angels Dedicated to Our Veterans and Troops.* All cookbooks are available through the Soldiers' Angels store (www.soldiersangels.org).

Disclaimers and Abbreviations Used

The recipes have been reproduced as submitted and we hope that all essential ingredients have been written down! Soldiers' Angels can not be responsible for errors in any recipe.

Standard abbreviations include:

- Cup(s) = c
- Gallon = gal
- Ounce = oz
- Pint = pt
- Quart = qt
- Tablespoon(s) = T
- Teaspoon(s) = t

Happy Cooking!
With love from Soldiers' Angels

America the Beautiful

Words by Katharine Lee Bates, Melody by Samuel Ward

O beautiful for spacious skies,
For amber waves of grain,
For purple mountain majesties
Above the fruited plain!
America! America!
God shed his grace on thee
And crown thy good with brotherhood
From sea to shining sea!

O beautiful for pilgrim feet
Whose stern impassioned stress
A thoroughfare of freedom beat
Across the wilderness!
America! America!
God mend thine every flaw,
Confirm thy soul in self-control,
Thy liberty in law!

O beautiful for patriot dream
That sees beyond the years
Thine alabaster cities gleam
Undimmed by human tears!
America! America!
God shed his grace on thee
And crown thy good with brotherhood
From sea to shining sea!

Alabama

Alabama Bar-B-Que Bean Corn Casserole for 24

4 chopped onions 4 chopped bell peppers 6 cans white corn, drained 6 cans chili without beans 2 cans kidney beans, drained 1 large can tomato sauce 1 lb grated cheese butter	Sauté onions and peppers in butter until translucent, and soft. Add corn, chili, and beans. Divide between two 3-quart casseroles. Top each casserole with 1/2 large can tomato sauce and 1/2 pound grated cheese. Bake at 325 for at least 2 hours.

Ginger Carpenter, a Soldiers' Angel in Birmingham, Alabama

Alabama Chocolate Pecan Jumbo Christmas Fudge Pie

1¼ c chocolate wafer crumbs ⅓ c butter; melted ½ c butter; softened ¾ c brown sugar 3 eggs 12 oz semisweet chocolate morsels 2 t instant coffee 1 t vanilla extract ½ c flour 1 c pecans; coarsely chopped whipped cream, sweetened chocolate syrup maraschino cherries with stems (optional) mint sprigs (optional)	Combine chocolate wafer crumbs and 1/3 cup melted butter; firmly press on bottom and sides of a 9-inch tart pan or pie plate. Bake at 350 for 6 to 8 minutes. Cream 1/2 cup softened butter; gradually add brown sugar with the electric mixer at medium speed until blended. Add the eggs, one at a time, beating after each addition. Stir in the melted chocolate, instant coffee, vanilla extract, flour, and chopped pecans. Pour into the prepared crust. Bake at 375 for 25 minutes. Remove from oven and cool completely on a rack. Before serving, pipe sweetened whipped cream on each piece and drizzle with chocolate syrup. Garnish with cherries and/or mint if desired.

Donna Allon (fefifauxfumgirl), a Soldiers' Angel in Alabama; Bonnie Hott, a Soldiers' Angel in Alabama

Down Home Mac and Cheese

4 c cooked elbow macaroni 4 c Cheddar cheese 3 beaten eggs ¾ c sour cream 4 T butter 1 c buttermilk salt and pepper to taste	Cook macaroni according to directions and drain. While still hot, add 3 cups of cheese and mix up. Put in casserole dish. In another bowl, mix milk, eggs, sour cream, and butter. Add salt and pepper. Pour over macaroni and blend. Top with remaining cup of cheese. Bake at 350 for 30 to 40 minutes. I cover for first 20 minutes and then uncover so top gets browned.

Bonnie Hott, a Soldiers' Angel in Alabama

Pimento Cheese Sandwich Filling

8 oz sharp Cheddar cheese, shredded 8 oz white Cheddar cheese, shredded or substitute 8 oz shredded pepper jack for a "kick") 1 small jar pimentos ¼ c mayonnaise ¼ c buttermilk ¼ c cup diced onions and pickle relish (optional)	Blend all ingredients. Can be used on sandwiches or crackers. Also used as a dip if thinned with a little more buttermilk.

Bonnie Hott, a Soldiers' Angel in Alabama

Redneck Caviar

2 (16-oz) cans black-eyed peas, drained 2 (11-oz) cans white shoepeg corn, drained 2 (11-oz) cans diced tomatoes and green chilies, undrained 2 large green bell peppers, chopped 12 small green onions, chopped 3 ripe tomatoes, chopped 1 t garlic powder 1 t garlic salt 1 t dried parsley flakes 1 (16-oz) large Italian dressing scoop-style corn chips, for serving	Combine all ingredients except dressing in a bowl, blending well. Pour dressing over all and toss well to coat. Refrigerate overnight. Serve with corn chips. This is yummy and good for you too! Use the fat-free Italian dressing and, other than the corn chips, this is a fat free snack!!

Lori, a Soldiers' Angel in Alabama

Sausage and Egg Pie

1 lb sausage meat 6 - 8 eggs 1 (9-inch) pie crust, unbaked	Cook sausage. Crumble sausage. Mix up eggs as you would for scrambled. Put crumbled sausage and shredded cheese to egg mixture. Pour in pie crust. Bake at 375 for 15 minutes or until eggs are done. You may substitute ham for sausage, and you can adjust sausage and eggs depending on how many pies you want.

Bonnie Hott, a Soldiers' Angel in Alabama

Alaska

Salmon Bake with Pecan Crunch Coating

2 T Dijon-style mustard 2 T melted butter 4 t honey ¼ c fresh bread crumbs ¼ c finely chopped pecans or walnuts 2 t chopped parsley 4 (4 - 6 oz each) Alaska Salmon fillets or steaks, thawed if necessary salt and black pepper lemon wedges, for serving	Mix mustard, butter, and honey in a small bowl; set aside. Mix bread crumbs, pecans, and parsley in a small bowl; set aside. Season each salmon fillet or steak with salt and pepper. Place on a lightly greased baking sheet or broiling pan. Brush each fillet or steak with mustard-honey mixture. Pat top of each fillet or steak with bread crumb mixture. Bake at 400 for 10 minutes per inch of thickness, measured at thickest part, or until salmon just flakes when tested with a fork. Serve with lemon wedges.

Donna Allon (fefifauxfumgirl), a Soldiers' Angel in Alabama

Smoked Salmon

4 c dark brown sugar 2½ c pickling salt 6 T pepper 2 T cayenne 3 T garlic powder	Cut up salmon filets and lay a layer in a large roasting pan. Cover with a quarter inch of the brine. Put down another layer and do the same. Cover the pan with foil and keep cold (as in refrigerate) overnight. Remove the salmon form the pan and rinse thoroughly with cold water. Fish needs to air dry so that a glaze forms and wait until the filet is dry. Put in 175 oven for at least 30 minutes, but it may take longer. This should smoke them thoroughly!

Iris Wilde, a Soldiers Angel in Wisconsin

Arizona

Chocolate Chili Con Carne

3 lb beef chuck
freshly ground black pepper
salt
½ t ground cinnamon, plus 1 t
1 t ground cumin, plus 2 t
2 T chili powder, plus 2 T
masa harina
½ c extra-virgin olive oil
¼ c lard
4 red onions, peeled and minced
6 cloves garlic, minced
4 jalapeño peppers, sliced thin with seeds, stems removed
¼ c tomato paste
2 t dried oregano
2 - 3 (12-oz) bottles beer
1 (12-oz) can diced tomato in juices
1 qt chicken stock
3 (12-oz) cans black beans
2 oz bittersweet chocolate, cut into large chunks

Cut the chuck into 2-inch pieces. Place the chuck in a large bowl. Season liberally with pepper (about 20 turns of the pepper grinder) and salt to taste. Season with 1/2 teaspoon cinnamon, 1 teaspoon cumin, and 2 tablespoons chili powder. Mix this well and coat the meat with the masa harina. Preheat a cast iron Dutch oven on the stove over medium high heat. Add the olive oil and then the meat in 1 layer. Leave it alone, without turning it, so the meat will brown and caramelize. Meanwhile, add the lard. As it browns, slowly turn each piece with tongs. Once all sides are caramelized, remove the meat from the pan with a slotted spoon and place on a cookie sheet to cool, leaving juices in the Dutch oven. Add the onions and garlic and sauté for 5 minutes over medium heat until they start to caramelize and get soft. Add the jalapeños and allow to cook for 2 more minutes until soft. Add the tomato paste. Add the remaining 2 teaspoons cumin, 1 teaspoon cinnamon, the oregano, and 2 heaping tablespoons chili powder. Add beer. Stir to incorporate everything. Add diced tomatoes, and stir. Add the reserved meat and chicken stock. Simmer for 1 1/2 hours until meat is tender. Strain juice from the black beans, add the beans to the chili pot and bring up to simmer. Add chunks of chocolate. Stir until it melts. Serve immediately or store in the refrigerator for 2 to 3 days.

Dave Johnson, a Soldiers' Angel in Phoenix, Arizona

Coffee-Marinated London Broil

1 c strong black coffee ⅓ c loosely packed brown sugar ½ c cider vinegar ¼ c chopped onion 3 cloves garlic, minced 1 T olive oil 1 t dry mustard powder 1 t ground black pepper 1 lb London Broil or flank steak	Prepare marinade by whisking together coffee, brown sugar, vinegar, onion, garlic, and pepper in a medium bowl. Place London Broil or steak in a glass bowl. Pour marinade over steak and turn to coat. Cover with plastic wrap and refrigerate for at least an hour. Spray grill with nonstick cooking spray and preheat to high direct heat. Remove meat from bowl, discard marinade. Grill 5 to 7 minutes on each side or until steak reaches desired degree of doneness. Transfer steak to cutting board and let rest for 5 minutes. Slice thinly across the grain of the meat and serve.

Dave Johnson, a Soldiers' Angel in Phoenix, Arizona

Desert Chili

2 T vegetable oil 3 garlic cloves, chopped 2 onions, chopped 1 green bell pepper, chopped 3 lb beef, chopped, not ground 1 t ground cumin 1 t ground oregano 3 T chili powder 10 tomatoes, peeled and chopped 2 jalapeño peppers (optional) 1 can beer	Heat oil in a large heavy skillet. Add garlic, onions, and green pepper. Sauté until soft, about 5 to 7 minutes. Add beef and lightly brown on all surfaces. Drain off some of the fat if a lot has accumulated. Lean beef trimmed of all fat should not have an excess amount, however. Add remaining ingredients and simmer for 1 hour or slightly longer. Put a cover on skillet during cooking time, and slightly tilt it so steam can escape. Check often and stir to prevent sticking. Skim off fat as it rises. Best if allowed to sit, tightly covered, for an hour after cooking is complete.

Donna Allon (fefifauxfumgirl), a Soldiers' Angel in Alabama

Gambas al Ajillo (Grilled Shrimp with Garlic)

¾ c olive oil 3 T freshly chopped thyme leaves 1½ T ancho chili powder 6 cloves garlic, coarsely chopped 24 large shrimp, shelled and deveined salt and freshly ground black pepper 3 cloves garlic, thinly sliced wooden skewers soaked in water	Heat the grill to medium. Whisk together 1/4 cup of the oil, 2 tablespoons of the thyme, ancho powder, and chopped garlic in a small bowl. Skewer the shrimp and brush with marinade. Place the remaining 1/2 cup of the oil in a small saucepan, add the sliced garlic and cook until the sliced garlic is lightly golden brown. Remove the garlic slices with a slotted spoon to a plate lined with paper towels. Reserve the oil. Increase the heat of the grill to high. Remove the shrimp from the marinade, season with salt and pepper and grill until golden brown on each side, about 1 1/2 minutes per side. Remove the shrimp from the skewers, transfer to a platter and drizzle with some of the reserved garlic oil and the garlic chips. Sprinkle with the remaining thyme and garnish with oregano leaves.

Dave Johnson, a Soldiers' Angel in Phoenix, Arizona

Grilled Chicken with Arugula Salad

¼ c freshly squeezed lemon juice 1 small shallot, chopped ¼ c pure olive oil ¼ t coarsely ground fresh black pepper 4 boneless, skinless, chicken breasts, pounded thinly salt and pepper ½ lb arugula 2 ripe beefsteak tomatoes, diced 1 small red onion, peeled, halved and thinly sliced 2 T red wine vinegar 2 T extra-virgin olive oil, plus additional for garnish lemon halves, for garnish	Whisk together lemon juice, shallot, olive oil, and black pepper in a large baking dish. Add the chicken, turn to coat and marinate in the refrigerator for 30 minutes. Preheat grill to high. Remove chicken from marinade, season with salt on both sides, and grill for 2 to 3 minutes per side or until golden brown and just cooked through. Combine arugula, tomatoes, and onions in a large bowl, toss with the vinegar and oil and season with salt and pepper, to taste. Place each paillard on a large plate, drizzle with extra-virgin olive oil and top with some of the arugula-tomato salad. Garnish with lemon halves.

Dave Johnson, a Soldiers' Angel in Phoenix, Arizona

Southwestern Pressed Burger Cuban-Style

1 lb ground chuck salt and freshly ground black pepper ½ c best quality mayonnaise 3 cloves roasted garlic, pureed ¼ c Dijon mustard 4 hamburger buns 4 slices thinly sliced smoked ham 8 slices thinly sliced Swiss cheese 2 dill pickles, sliced into ¼-inch thick slices	Form the meat into 4 (¼-inch thick) burgers. Season the meat with salt and pepper on both sides and cook in a sauté pan over high heat to medium doneness, about 2 to 3 minutes per side. Combine the mayonnaise and roasted garlic in a small bowl and season with salt and pepper, to taste. Spread both sides of each bun with mayonnaise and mustard. Place a slice of cheese on the bottom portion of each bun, place the burger on top of the cheese, then top the burger with a slice of ham then another slice of cheese then the pickle slices. Place the tops of the bun over the pickles and cook on a sandwich press or wrap the burgers in aluminum foil and cook in a hot skillet over high heat with a heavy skillet placed on top of the burger to press the sandwich. Cook until golden brown and cheese has melted.

Dave Johnson, a Soldiers' Angel in Phoenix, Arizona

Tingalings

12 oz white chocolate 1 c salted peanuts 1½ c chow mein noodles	Melt chocolate over low heat stirring continuously. Add peanuts and noodles. Mix and drop by spoonfuls on waxed paper (or whatever you have). Store in refrigerator. Very easy to make and send to our troops.

Pam Butcher, a Soldiers' Angel in Yuma, Arizona

Arkansas

Arkansas Fish Fry

2 lb catfish
3 medium eggs
2 T milk or water
cornmeal or flour

Green Tomato Relish
6 large green tomatoes
1 red bell pepper, seeded
1 green pepper, seeded
4 large onions
1 T celery seed
1 T mustard seed
1 t salt
¾ c vinegar (or to taste)
1¾ c sugar (or to taste)

Rinse catfish. In a bowl, mix eggs with milk or water. Put ½ cup cornmeal into a plastic bag. Dip fish into egg/milk mixture and then into baggy with cornmeal; shake to cover. Fry in hot oil for about 5 to 10 minutes. Serve with hush puppies, green tomato relish, cole slaw, and beans of your choice.

For relish: Coarsely grind tomatoes, peppers, and onion. Drain this mixture and set aside. Combine tomato mixture, celery seed, mustard seed, salt, sugar, and vinegar. Bring to a boil and simmer over low heat 5 minutes, stirring frequently. Sterilize enough jars and lids to hold relish (4 one-pint jars, or 2 one-quart jars). Pack relish into sterilized jars, making sure there are no spaces or air pockets. Fill jars up and screw on lids. Keep jars apart by about 2 inches. Bring to full boil and process 30 minutes. Store up to a year.

Iris Wilde, a Soldiers' Angel in Wisconsin

Escalloped Pineapple

4 hot dog buns
1 (20-oz) can pineapple chunks in juice
3 eggs
1 stick butter
1 stick margarine
1¾ c sugar (can reduce to 1½ c)

Melt butter and margarine and mix with eggs and sugar. Drain pineapple chunks (drain well). Break apart hot dog buns. Mix hot dog bun pieces with pineapple chunks. Place pineapple and bun mixture in a 2-quart baking pan and pour remaining ingredients over mixture. DO NOT STIR. Bake 30 minutes at 350 or until bubbly. Can also be baked in the microwave. Serve warm. Makes for either a side dish or a dessert. You can serve as a dessert using individual dishes (sprinkle with cinnamon).

Mrs Gaye Cypert, Springdale, Arkansas

Peanut Brittle

1 c sugar ½ c light corn syrup ½ c water 1 c raw peanuts 1 t vanilla 1 t soda	Combine sugar, light corn syrup, and water in a heavy bottom skillet (cast iron if you have one). Cook over medium-high heat stirring often. Have a bowl of cold water near the stove. When the mixture begins to boil and turns golden brown, drop a ½ teaspoon of the mixture into the cold water. If the syrup immediately hardens into a brittle string or ball, add the raw peanuts to the mixture, stir, add the vanilla to the mixture, stir, then add the soda to the mixture, stir and then immediately pour onto the cookie sheet. Allow the mixture to settle, cool, and harden. Once cool, break into pieces and enjoy.

Mrs Ila Mae Graves, Abbott, Arkansas

Stuffed Portobellos

4 (4-inch) Portobello mushrooms ½ c sliced green onion 1 clove garlic, minced ¼ c butter ⅔ c fine dry bread crumbs ½ c finely shredded Parmigiano-Reggiano cheese 1 T snipped fresh sage 1 T dry white wine or vermouth ¼ t freshly ground black pepper ½ c chicken broth fresh sage leaves Parmigiano-Reggiano cheese for garnish	Rinse mushrooms and remove stems. Drain mushrooms on paper towels. Finely chop stems to equal 1 cup. In saucepan, cook chopped stems, green onion, and garlic in butter over medium heat for 2 minutes. Remove from heat. Stir in bread crumbs, ½ cup cheese, 1 tablespoon sage, wine or vermouth, and pepper. Place mushroom caps, stem side up, in a shallow roasting pan. Divide stuffing mixture among mushrooms. Pour broth around mushrooms in pan. Bake at 400 for 15 minutes or until mushrooms are tender and filling is heated through. Garnish with fresh sage and shards of cheese. Serve whole or slice each mushroom into halves.

Mrs Julie Roblee, Fayetteville, Arkansas

White Chocolate Fudge (Girls' Fudge)

2 (6 sq each) pkg white chocolate ¾ c sweetened condensed milk 1 c chopped pecans 1 c dried cranberries 1 t orange extract 1 T grated orange peel	Line an 8-inch square pan with foil Microwave chocolate and milk in a large bowl until chocolate is almost melted. Stir until smooth. Add rest of ingredients and blend well. Spread in prepared pan. Refrigerate 2 hours or until firm. Store in tightly covered container in refrigerator 2 to 3 weeks.

Debby Shaw, a Soldiers' Angel in Fort Smith, Arkansas

California

Angel Date Drops

2 egg whites ¼ t salt 1 t vanilla ¾ c sugar ½ c cut-up dates 1 c chopped pecans 1 T flour	Beat egg whites with salt and vanilla until soft peaks form. Gradually beat in sugar, beating until stiff peaks form. Sprinkle dates and nuts with the flour; toss. Fold into egg whites. Drop by teaspoonfuls about 2 inches apart on greased cookie sheet. Bake at 350 for 10 to 12 minutes. Makes about 3 dozen meringue cookies.

Terri Carter, a Soldiers' Angel in Palm Springs, California

Avocado-Coconut Ice Cream

1½ c milk (or half-and-half) 1 c sweet coconut cream ⅓ c white sugar 2 (½ lb) avocados, peeled and pitted ¾ t lemon juice 1 t vanilla	Purée milk, coconut cream, sugar, avocados, and lemon juice in a blender until smooth. Pour into a bowl, cover, and refrigerate for several hours until cold. Freeze in an ice cream machine according to manufacturer's directions, and then freeze overnight. Allow ice cream to soften in refrigerator for 10 minutes before serving. If you don't have an ice cream machine, you can make this in the freezer. Just pour the puree into a dish and place it into the freezer. Freeze for 2 to 3 hours, then mash it into a slush consistency; repeat the freezing and mashing about 3 to 4 times so that the ice cream will be smooth. Finally, freeze overnight and serve as directed.

Carrie Ann, a Soldiers' Angel in Malibu, California

Banana Bread

2 ripe bananas ¾ c water 3 c white granulated sugar 4 eggs ⅔ c vegetable oil 1 t nutmeg 1 t cinnamon 1½ t salt 2 t baking soda 3 c flour butter, for serving	Preheat oven to 350. In a small mixing bowl, mash the bananas and blend with the water. Set aside. In a larger mixing bowl, mix (at low speed) the sugar, oil, eggs, nutmeg, cinnamon, and salt. Add and mix in salt, banana and water mixture, baking soda, and flour in this order. Grease and flour 2 loaf pans generously. Fill each about 2/3 full with batter. Bake at 350 for 1 hour. During baking, DO NOT open the oven to check on the loaves. Let the loaves bake for a full hour, they will appear very dark. Use the toothpick test, and if there is a little uncooked batter on the toothpick, let the loaves cook for another 2 to 3 minutes. When done, take them out and let cool for 5 to 10 minutes. Turn the loaves out and finish cooling. Wrap and store in the refrigerator, or freeze. This bread is yummiest when served warm with butter.

Shannon Lawrence, a Soldiers' Angel in La Verne, California

Bachelor Quarters Beef Stew

3 T oil 2 lb stew meat ½ c chopped green pepper 1 c diced potatoes 1 c sliced carrots ½ c chopped celery 1 c sliced onion ½ t salt 1 large clove garlic ⅛ t pepper 1 small can mushrooms 1 (8-oz) can tomatoes 3 c beef stock 3 T cornstarch (or use flour) ⅓ c barbecue sauce (or catsup) ¼ c cold water	Sauté onion, pepper and garlic in oil. Add salt, pepper, barbecue sauce, tomatoes, potatoes, carrots, celery, beef stock and mushrooms. Add the stew meat to the crock pot, cover with mixture. Cook on low for 8 to 10 hours. Mix cornstarch and cold water, add to crock pot to thicken before serving.

Robin Lynne, a Soldiers' Angel in Penngrove, California

Clam Dip

3 cans minced clams 3 pkg cream cheese 2 T white wine Worcestershire sauce or 1 T wine and 1 T regular Worcestershire sauce 2 large round unsliced Shepard's or sour dough bread	Soften cream cheese and add clams, wine, and Worcestershire sauce. Slice off top of one bread to create a lid, set lid aside. Carefully remove center of the bread round well to make a place for the dip. Slice center of first and entire second bread round into 1-inch cubes. Put bread lid on and wrap in tin foil and place on cooking sheet. Bake for 2 hours at 350. Stir before serving. This is a wonderful family treat. Cowabunga, Dude!

Patti Patton-Bader, founder of Soldiers' Angels

Cocoa Roll

2 rounded T cocoa 2 rounded T flour 6 T sugar 4 egg yolks 1 T water (optional) 4 egg whites beaten stiff ½ pt whipping cream powdered sugar	This great dessert recipe has been in our family for over 50 years. It's quick, easy and fabulous....Preheat oven to 400. In a small bowl, stir together cocoa, flour, and sugar. Add egg yolks to dry ingredients and stir (if too dry, add 1 tablespoon water); set aside. Fold egg whites into the chocolate mixture. Don't over mix! It should be a frothy mixture. Spread on nonstick cookie sheet. Bake 10 minutes or until done. Cool. Whip the cream, sweetening it to taste. Loosen edge of cooled cocoa roll with spatula. Spread on whipped cream and roll, using spatula to loosen as you go along. Sprinkle powdered sugar over the top (if your roll isn't perfect, that will cover all the flaws). Left onto oval serving plate and slice. In the summer, try ice cream instead of whipping cream and serve with a little hot fudge on each slice with a floweret of whipped cream.

Betty Higgins, a Very Special Soldiers' Angel in Manhattan Beach, California

Fig Raisin Spice Muffins/Cake

1 c chopped fresh figs 1 c raisins 2 c all-purpose flour 2 t baking powder 2 t cinnamon ½ t nutmeg ¼ t allspice ¼ t salt boiling water ½ c solid shortening 1 c brown sugar, packed 2 eggs, beaten	You can make this as a cake using a loaf pan, or an 8- or 9-inch square pan or as muffins. Reduce the baking time accordingly by using the toothpick method. Preheat oven to 375. Grease a standard loaf pan. Cover figs and raisins with boiling water and let sit to plump for 15 minutes. Drain thoroughly and pat dry with paper towels. In a medium bowl, whisk together flour, baking powder, cinnamon, nutmeg, allspice and salt. Set aside. In a large bowl, cream shortening and brown sugar together until fluffy. Beat in eggs. Add flour mixture, half at a time, to the wet ingredients. Blend until smooth and combined. Fold in figs and raisins. Pour into prepared pan and bake for 35 to 40 minutes. Let cool to room temperature before slicing to serve.

Carrie Ann, a Soldiers' Angel in Malibu, California

Garlow's Healthy Date Cookies

4 c rolled oats 1 (15-oz) can cannelloni beans, drained and rinsed ½ c white sugar ½ c brown sugar 1 t vanilla extract 1 t baking powder 1 t baking soda 1 t ground cinnamon ½ c chopped pitted dates ½ c flaked coconut ½ c dried cranberries ½ c cherries ½ c chopped walnuts ½ c applesauce ½ c skim milk 2 egg whites	Preheat the oven to 325. Grease cookie sheets. Grind the oats in a blender until resembling coarse flour. Puree beans and applesauce to a smooth paste. Stir in the white sugar, brown sugar and vanilla, skim milk and egg whites; blend well. Combine the ground oats, baking powder, baking soda, and cinnamon; blend into the bean mixture. Stir in the dates, coconut, cranberries, cherries, and walnuts. Drop dough by heaping spoonfuls onto the prepared cookie sheet. Bake for 15 to 18 minutes in the preheated oven, until golden. Cool on baking sheets for 5 minutes then remove to wire racks to cool completely.

Carrie Ann, a Soldiers' Angel in Malibu, California

Gina's Burrito Bar

6 (double) chicken breasts (boneless, skinless) 1 (16-oz) jar salsa (any heat you wish) 3 cans black beans (drain the juice) sour cream, guacamole, onions, salsa, shredded cheese, olives, etc for burrito bar	This recipe is for 10 to 12 people but it can be adapted to serve 50 to 100. Put all ingredients into crock pot and cook all day. Take meat out of juice and shred. Add juice to mixture. Put in bowl.

Judy McDaniel, a Soldiers' Angel in Napa, California

Lemon Pasta

½ stick sweet (unsalted) butter 1 c heavy cream 4 T freshly squeezed lemon juice 1 lb fresh pasta or noodles, fine ones are best 2 t freshly grated lemon zest freshly ground black pepper and freshly grated Parmesan cheese, for serving	In southern California, we just walk into the backyard and pick a lemon for dinner. Melt butter in a saucepan. Add heavy cream and freshly squeezed lemon juice. Do not heat beyond the point where the chill is off the cream. Remove from the heat and cover to keep warm. Cook fresh pasta or noodles and drain, saving ½ cup of the pasta water. Add the pasta and freshly grated lemon zest to the sauce pan. Add 2 tablespoons of pasta water (add more if necessary). Serve in bowls with lots of freshly ground black pepper and freshly grated Parmesan cheese.

MaryAnn Foote, a Soldiers' Angel in Westlake Village, California

London Broil Marinade

½ c vegetable oil ½ c soy sauce ½ T lemon juice onion flakes dash of garlic	Mix all ingredients and use with London broil.

Jan Sietsema, a Soldiers' Angel in Chatsworth, California

Low-fat California Date Shakes

1 c chopped, pitted California dates 1 c 1% milk or skim milk 1 ripe banana 1 (8-oz) container low-fat vanilla yogurt 1 c crushed ice	In a blender, combine the dates, milk, banana, yogurt, and ice and blend for 1 minute or 2 minutes until frothy and thick. Then enjoy a great treat! Yield: 2 servings unless someone likes more than others...

Terri Carter, a Soldiers' Angel in Palm Springs, California

Malibu Energy Bar

1½ c granola ½ c almonds, halved ½ c miniature M & M candies ½ c dried currants 1 c dried prunes ½ c dried apricots ¼ c dried cranberries	Line a baking sheet with wax paper. Set aside. In a large bowl, combine granola, peanuts, candies and currants. Set aside. In a food processor, combine prunes, apricots and cranberries. Process until smooth. Add processed fruit to granola mixture. Mix well. From about 1/3 cup mixture into a tightly packed 4 x 1 ½ x 3/4-inch bar. Place bar on prepared baking sheet. Repeat with remaining mixture. Let bars air-dry overnight on the counter. Store bars in airtight container between sheets of wax paper. Makes 10 bars. Note: Substitute miniature chocolate chips for M&Ms. Also try 1 cup of sunflower flower seeds in the mix! Yummy!!

Carrie Ann, a Soldiers' Angel in Malibu, California

Marinated Drummettes

2 - 4 pkg chicken drummettes or wings (about 14 per pkg) ½ c butter or margarine 1 c brown sugar 1 c soy sauce ¾ c water 1 t dry mustard	Melt the butter or margarine. Mix in brown sugar, soy sauce, water, and dry mustard. Pour over chicken, marinate. If there isn't time, don't marinate. Bake 1 to 1 ½ hours at 350. A glass baking dish is best to use.

Jan Sietsema, a Soldiers' Angel in Chatsworth, California

Mexican Margarita Bars

30 saltines 1 c flour 1 c powdered sugar ½ c sweet butter, softened 4 eggs 1½ c sugar ¼ c lime juice (fresh is best) 2 T plus 5 t orange-flavored liqueur 1 t grated lime zest	Heat oven to 350. In food processor, grind saltines into crumbs. Add flour and ½ cup powdered sugar. Pulse. Add butter and process until mixture forms a mass. Press into a 9-inch square baking dish lined with greased aluminum foil. Bake 20 minutes or until edges are golden. Beat eggs, sugar, lime juice and zest, and 2 tablespoons liqueur until well blended. Pour over crust. Bake 20 to 25 minutes or until set. Cool. Combine ½ c powdered sugar and 5 teaspoons liqueur. Spread over cooled cookie. Cut into 64 bars.

Jayne Brown, a Soldiers' Angel in California

Pronto Enchilada Casserole

1 lb hamburger ½ onion, chopped 1 clove garlic or use powdered chili powder to taste ½ t oregano salt to taste 1 (14-oz) can enchilada sauce (medium or hot) large flour corn tortillas small can chopped olives (optional) 1 - 1 ½ c shredded Cheddar cheese	Brown hamburger, drain, and add onion and spices. Add ½ can enchilada sauce, and simmer until thick. Dip tortillas in remaining sauce, layer baking dish with tortillas, meat, olives, and cheese. Repeat, ending with tortilla and cheese. Bake for 30 minutes at 350. Easy and tasty.

Jan Sietsema, a Soldiers' Angel in Chatsworth, California

Spicy Tofu with Apricots

1 block firm tofu 3 T soy sauce 1 T balsamic vinegar 1 T dry sherry 1 t sesame seeds 2 t curry powder or garam masala 2 t chili oil 1 T sugar 1 t dried chives, or 2 sliced fresh chives 1 t dried parsley or 2 T fresh, chopped 2 T olive oil 1 clove garlic, minced 1 medium onion, chopped 1 large carrot cut on diagonal ¼ c chopped peanuts or almonds 6 – 8 fresh apricots, sliced or ¼ c chopped dried apricots ¼ - ½ c apricot preserves udon, for serving	Cut block of tofu into 16 cubes. Put into a ceramic dish or Ziploc bag. Mix soy sauce, vinegar, sherry, sesame seeds, curry powder, chili oil, sugar, chives, and parsley. Pour over tofu in dish or bag. Marinate at least 1 hour; longer is better. Heat oil in large skillet or wok. Add garlic, onion, carrot, nuts, and apricots; stir fry until onion is soft. Add tofu and its marinade. Add preserves. Cook until brown and 'sticky'. Serve over udon.

MaryAnn Foote, a Soldiers' Angel in Westlake Village, California

Colorado

Beef, Beans, and Biscuits

Ingredients	Instructions
1 lb ground beef 2 green onions, chopped 1 garlic clove, minced 1 (29-oz) can baked beans, drained ½ c barbeque sauce ¼ c packed brown sugar ¼ c ketchup 1 T prepared mustard 1 (4½-oz) tube refrigerated buttermilk biscuits ½ c shredded cheese	In a large skillet, cook the ground beef, onions, and garlic, over medium heat until meat is no longer pink. Drain. Add the beans, barbeque sauce, brown sugar, ketchup, and mustard. Simmer for 5 minutes or until heated through. Transfer to a greased 11 x 7 x 2 baking dish. Separate biscuits and cut in half; arrange over beef mixture. Bake, uncovered, at 400 for 18 minutes or until biscuits are golden brown. Sprinkle with cheese; bake 2 to 3 minutes longer or until cheese is melted.

Christine Kuhn, a Soldiers' Angel in Greeley, Colorado

Calabacitas Casserole with Polenta and Cheese

Ingredients	Instructions

3 T extra-virgin olive oil
2 c corn kernels, defrosted
4 cloves garlic, smashed
1 green chili pepper seeded and chopped
    or 2 jalapeños, seeded and chopped
2 small - medium zucchini, diced
1 small - medium yellow squash, diced
1 large yellow onion, chopped
1 (14-oz) can stewed tomatoes
2 t dark chili powder
salt and pepper
1 (16-oz) tube prepared polenta
2 c shredded Monterey Jack
3 scallions, chopped
2 T chopped cilantro leaves or flat-leaf
    parsley
	Preheat oven to 500. Heat a large skillet over medium high heat. Add 2 tablespoons olive oil, corn, garlic, and chilies. Sauté 3 minutes, add zucchini and yellow squash and onions, season with salt and pepper, chili powder; cook 7 to 8 minutes. Add stewed tomatoes and heat through. Transfer to baking dish, oiled with 1 tablespoon of olive oil. Cut 1 tube of polenta in 1/2-inch slices lengthwise. Top vegetables with polenta and cheese. Place in hot oven to melt cheese and warm polenta, 8 to 10 minutes. Garnish with chopped scallions and cilantro or flat-leaf parsley.

Jenn Page, a Soldiers' Angel in Buena Vista, Colorado

Chili for a Crowd

3 lb ground beef 2 (28-oz) cans kidney beans, rinsed and drained 1 lb smoked kielbasa, sliced and halved 2 large onions, halved and thinly sliced 2 (8-oz) cans tomato sauce ⅔ c hickory-flavored barbeque sauce 1½ c water ½ c packed brown sugar 3 fresh jalapeño peppers, seeded and sliced 2 T chili powder 2 t ground mustard 2 t coffee granules 1 t EACH dried oregano, thyme, and sage ½ t cayenne pepper 2 garlic cloves, minced	In an 8-quart kettle or Dutch oven, cook beef over medium heat until beef is no longer pink. Drain. Add the remaining ingredients and bring to a boil. Reduce the heat: cover and simmer for 1 hour, stirring occasionally. 20 servings

Christine Kuhn, a Soldiers' Angel in Greeley, Colorado

Corn Chowder

2 T margarine or butter ¼ c onion, chopped 1 medium peeled and diced potato 1 (15-oz) can whole kernel corn, drained (save the liquid you will use it later) ½ t salt ¼ t pepper 2 T flour 2 c milk	Sauté onion in the margarine or butter until tender. Add potato, corn liquid, and salt. Cook over medium heat for 15 minutes or until potato is almost tender. Add corn and salt and pepper. Stir flour into a small amount of the milk and mix until smooth. Add to corn mixture. Add remaining milk. Cook, stirring constantly for 5 minutes, until potatoes are cooked and chowder thickens slightly. Serve hot. Christine's note: I also like to put any leftover ham that I have in this chowder. If you do that increase the milk slightly.

Christine Kuhn, a Soldiers' Angel in Greeley, Colorado

Dilly Dip

1 pkg (1-oz) dry ranch dressing mix 1 c mayonnaise 1 c sour cream 1½ t dried dill 1½ c radishes, coarsely chopped 2 T onion, finely chopped 1 medium carrot, grated	In 1-quart bowl, combine dressing mix, mayonnaise, sour cream, and dill. Mix well. Stir in vegetables. Chill and serve.

Judy Offner, a Soldiers' Angel in Littleton, Colorado

Farmer's Breakfast

15 oz (about 4½ c) frozen hash browns, thawed spray butter or about 2 T melted butter 8 eggs 1 c half-and-half 1 t dried parsley 1 t chopped chives ½ t salt ½ t pepper 2 c (8 oz) shredded Colby cheese 6 oz (about 1 c) Canadian bacon or ham, chopped tomato slices, for garnish cilantro sprigs, for garnish	Preheat oven to 400. Coat a 9 inch deep-dish pie plate with nonstick cooking spray. Press thawed hash browns between paper towels to remove excess moisture. Place hash browns into prepared pie plate and press to form an even, solid crust on the bottom and sides of the pie plate. Spray potatoes evenly with the spray butter or the melted butter. Bake the crust for 20 minutes. Meanwhile, in a large bowl beat together the eggs, half-and-half, dried parsley, chives, salt and pepper. After removing the potato crust from the oven, sprinkle the cheese on top of the potatoes and add over with the Canadian bacon or ham. Give the egg mixture another stir to thoroughly mix the ingredients and pour all ingredients in the pie plate. Lower oven temperature to 350. Bake for 45 minutes, or until set. Let the quiche stand for about 10 minutes before slicing. Garnish plates with sliced tomatoes and sprigs of cilantro. Note: Put the hash browns in the refrigerator overnight between layers of paper towels, and they will be ready to go in the morning.

Christine Kuhn, a Soldiers' Angel in Greeley, Colorado

Strawberries and Cream Muffins

½ c butter, room temperature 1 c sugar 2 large eggs, beaten ½ c sour cream 2 t vanilla extract 1⅔ c all purpose flour 2 t baking powder 1 c chopped fresh strawberries	Preheat oven to 375. Grease the cups of a muffin tin or use paper liners (12). In a large bowl, cream the butter and sugar. Add the beaten eggs, sour cream, and vanilla. Sift the flour and baking powder together; gradually stir into wet ingredients. Gently fold in the strawberries. The dough will be somewhat stiff. DO NOT OVER MIX OR THE MUFFINS WILL BE TOUGH. Spoon the batter into the muffin cups. Bake for 20 minutes, or until the tops of the muffins are lightly springy and slightly brown. Let cool for 5 minutes before turning the muffins onto a wire rack. These are good warm or cold.

Christine Kuhn, a Soldiers' Angel in Greeley, Colorado

Posse Soup

2 lb ground beef 1 large onion, chopped 2 cloves garlic 1 large can ranch-style beans, undrained 2 cans corn, undrained 2 cans hominy (one each white and yellow), undrained 1 small can chopped green chilies, undrained 1 qt tomatoes, undrained 1 t basil salt and pepper to taste	Brown ground beef, onions, garlic, salt, and pepper. Drain meat mixture and add remaining ingredients, juice and all with each can. Simmer about 1 hour. Enough for the whole posse!

Judy Offner, a Soldiers' Angel in Littleton, Colorado

Connecticut

Bread & Butter Pickles

1 gal cucumbers 8 small onions, shredded 2 green peppers, shredded ½ c salt 4 c sugar ½ t turmeric ½ t ground cloves 2 T mustard seed 1 t celery seed 3 c white vinegar 2 c water	Wash and thinly slice cucumbers. Layer cucumbers, onions and peppers. Sprinkle salt on each layer and cover with ice. Let stand for 3 hours to overnight. Drain chilled cucumbers. Mix sugar, spices, vinegar, and water. Boil to make a syrup. Pour syrup over cucumbers, place over slow heat and heat to scalding (not boil) stirring occasionally with wooden spoon. Seal while hot in sterilized jars.

Martha Burbridge, a Soldiers' Angel in Union, Connecticut

Grandma's Crumb Cake

⅔ c butter 2 c flour 2 t baking powder 2 eggs 1½ c sugar ½ t salt ¾ c milk 1 t vanilla	Mix butter, sugar, flour, salt. and baking powder with fingers. Set aside ½ cup to spread over batter. Add to the remaining mixture milk, eggs, and vanilla. Beat well with electric beater. Pour batter into greased 9-inch pan. Sprinkle topping set aside over top. Bake at 350 for 30 minutes.

Martha Burbridge, a Soldiers' Angel in Union, Connecticut

Happiness (Ladies Benevolent Association, Union, CT [1926])

Take 1 ounce of work, mix well with patience. Pour in 1 cup of love and 1 cup of sympathy. Stir well with the spoon of understanding. Sift in 1 cup of humor. Bake thoroughly in an atmosphere of loyalty and trust.

Martha Burbridge, a Soldiers' Angel in Union, Connecticut

Orange Waffles

1 c flour 1 T sugar ¼ t salt 1½ t baking powder ⅛ t nutmeg 2 eggs ½ c milk rind of an orange, coarsely grated 2 T butter, melted	Mix dry ingredients and let sit at room temperature for 1/2 hour. Mix wet ingredients, except for melted butter, and let sit at room temperature for 1/2 hour. Add the dry ingredients to the wet ingredients. Beat until the waffle batter is smooth. Add the 2 tablespoons of melted butter to the batter and mix until fully combined. Follow manufacturer's instructions for waffle iron operation. Pour/spoon 1/2 to 3/4 cup of batter onto preheated waffle iron sections. Bake at a high heat until waffles turn golden brown. Caution: do not overbake, as the timing on many waffle irons will overcook the waffle when cooked at high heat.

Cherilyn Brown, a Soldiers' Angel in Lithia Springs, Georgia

Rocky Road Peanut Butter Cups

1⅔ c peanut butter and milk chocolate cups (11-oz pkg) 2 T smooth peanut butter 1 c crispy rice cereal 1 c miniature marshmallows ¾ c chopped unsalted dry roasted peanuts	Microwave peanut butter and milk chocolate cups in a large glass bowl on HIGH for 2 minutes or until melted, stirring every 30 seconds. Stir in peanut butter. Stir in cereal, marshmallows, and peanuts. Spoon mixture evenly into 36 miniature paper candy cups. Chill for 1 hour or until firm.

Jen Reeser, a Soldiers Angel in Avon, Connecticut

Un-Swedish Meatballs

1 lb ground chicken or turkey 1 can condensed cream of celery soup ½ can milk rice or noodles, for serving	Mix milk and condensed soup in casserole. Add meatballs made from ground meat. Cook in microwave for 10 minutes, stir and cook for 5 more minutes. Serve over noodles or rice.

Martha Burbridge, a Soldiers' Angel in Union, Connecticut

Delaware

Angel Cake Supreme

1 c sifted cake flour 1½ c (12) egg whites 1¼ c sifted confectioners sugar 1½ t cream of tartar ¼ t almond extract ¼ t salt 1 c sugar 1½ t vanilla	Sift flour and confectioners sugar together 3 times. Beat egg whites with cream of tartar, salt, vanilla, and almond extract with an electric mixer, until stiff enough to hold up in soft peaks, but still moist and glossy. Beat in the granulated sugar, 2 tablespoons at a time, continue to beat until the meringue holds stiff peaks. Sift about 1/4 of the flour mixture over the egg white meringue; fold in lightly with an up-and-down-and-over motion, turning the bowl as you go. Fold in the remaining flour by fourths. Mix well, but do not over stir! Bake in an ungreased angel food cake pan at 375 for 30 minutes or until done. Invert the pan and cool the cake thoroughly.

Lisa Borkoski, a Soldiers' Angel in Seaford, Delaware

Cheesy Chicken Enchiladas

1 medium onion, chopped 2 T margarine 1½ c cooked chicken (or turkey) 1 (12-oz) jar picante sauce ½ pkg cream cheese 1 T ground cumin 2 c shredded Cheddar cheese 8 (6-inch) flour tortillas	Heat oven to 350. Cut chicken into strips. Melt margarine in a large skillet and cook onions until tender. Stir in chicken, 1/4 cup picante sauce, cream cheese, and cumin. Cook until thoroughly heated. Stir in 1 cup cheese. Spoon about 1/3 cup chicken mixture in center of each tortilla; roll up. Place seam side down in 12 x 7 inch baking dish (sprayed with cooking spray). Top with remaining picante sauce and cheese. Bake 15 minutes.

Farrah Morelli, a Soldiers' Angel in Delmar, Delaware

Ham Balls

1 lb precooked ham (ground to a hamburger consistency) 2 c milk 2 lb ground beef 1 t salt 2 c graham cracker crumbs 1 can tomato soup 2 eggs ½ c vinegar 1 c brown sugar	Mix the 2 meats, graham cracker crumbs, eggs, milk, and salt and shape into balls. Mix the sauce: tomato soup, vinegar, and brown sugar. Pour the sauce over the meatballs. Bake at 350 for 1 1/2 hours.

Lisa Borkoski, a Soldiers' Angel in Seaford, Delaware

Leftover Lasagna

mashed potatoes sliced turkey or chicken corn stuffing	Using an oven-safe pan layer, your holiday leftovers. I start with the mashed potatoes; then add turkey/chicken; followed by corn; and topped with stuffing. Warm in oven (I use 350) for 10 to 15 minutes.

Courtney, a Soldiers' Angel in Delaware

Mexican Hot Dish

1 lb ground beef 1 - 2 T brown sugar 1 t garlic powder 1 T cornmeal 1 T dry minced onion 1 (15-oz) can chili beans (not drained) ½ t taco seasoning 1½ c shredded Cheddar cheese 1 (8-oz) can tomato sauce 2 c corn chips (crushed) ½ c taco sauce 1 c sour cream ¾ c water	In a large skillet, brown meat and drain off fat. Add garlic powder, onion, taco seasoning, tomato sauce, taco sauce, water, and brown sugar. Simmer 15 minutes. Then stir in the corn meal. Add the chili beans and stir in half of the cheese and half of the corn chips. Pour into a greased casserole dish and bake at 350 for 25 minutes. Spread sour cream over top and sprinkle with the remaining corn chips, then the remaining cheese. Bake for 5 more minutes until the cheese is melted.

Lisa Borkoski, a Soldiers' Angel in Seaford, Delaware

Oatmeal Cake

1 c quick oatmeal 1½ c boiling water 1 ½ c flour 1 c white sugar 1 t baking soda 2 c brown sugar ½ t cinnamon ½ c shortening (I use softened butter) 1 t salt 2 eggs ½ c shredded coconut ¼ c milk ½ c chopped walnuts or pecans	Combine oatmeal and boiling water. Let stand. Mix flour, white sugar, baking soda, 1 cup brown sugar, cinnamon, shortening, salt, and eggs. Add the oatmeal mixture; blend well. Bake at 350 for 35 minutes. Mix 1 c brown sugar, coconut, milk, and nuts and spread on the warm cake. Bake 10 minutes longer. Eat warm or cool.

Lisa Borkoski, a Soldiers' Angel in Seaford, Delaware

Pretzel Salad

2 c crushed pretzels (put in plastic baggie and roll with rolling pin) ¾ c melted butter 4 T sugar 1 c sugar 1 (8-oz) pkg cream cheese 1 (8-oz) container frozen dessert topping 1 large box strawberry gelatin 1¾ c boiling water 2 (10-oz) pkg frozen strawberries	Mix pretzels, butter, and 4 tablespoons sugar. Press into a 9 x 13 inch baking dish and bake at 375 for 8 minutes. Cream together 1 cup sugar, cream cheese, and thawed dessert topping. Pour over the crust and spread it out. Mix gelatin, boiling water, and strawberries. When it starts to set up, pour over the top and refrigerate. When solid, cut into squares and serve.

Donya, a Soldiers' Angel in Middletown, Delaware

Red, White, and Blue Salad

2 boxes red raspberry gelatin 1 pkg plain gelatin ½ c half-and-half milk 1 c white sugar 1 t vanilla 8 oz softened cream cheese ½ c chopped walnuts 1 (21-oz) can blueberry pie filling	Dissolve 1 box red raspberry gelatin in 2 cups boiling water. Chill in a 9 x 13 inch pan until set. Dissolve plain gelatin in 1/2 cup cold water. Mix together with 1/2 cup of half-and-half. Heat, but do not boil. Add white sugar and vanilla. Remove from heat and add softened cream cheese. Stir until cream cheese is dissolved. Add chopped walnuts. Gently pour over first layer and chill until set. Dissolve second box of raspberry geltain in 1 cup of boiling water. Stir in blueberry pie filling. Gently pour over second layer and chill until set.

Lisa Borkoski, a Soldiers' Angel in Seaford, Delaware

Florida

30-minute Chicken and Wild Rice Soup

5⅔ c water 1 pkg long grain and wild rice mix (with seasoning pack) 1 pkg dehydrated chicken noodle soup 1 large stalk celery, sliced 1 medium carrot, sliced (I add extra carrots) ⅓ c onion, chopped 2 cans condensed cream of chicken soup (do not dilute) 1 c cooked chicken breast	In a large saucepan, combine water, rice with contents of seasoning packet, and dry soup mix. Bring to a boil. Reduce heat; cover and simmer for 10 minutes. Stir in celery, carrot, and onion. Cover and simmer for 10 minutes. Stir in cream of chicken soup and chicken. Cook 8 minutes longer or until rice and vegetables are tender.

jmsblue, a Soldiers' Angel in Florida

Chicken Pot Pie

2 pie crusts 1 can of mixed vegetables 1 can cream of mushroom soup 3 boneless chicken breasts	Preheat oven to 350. Cook chicken breast and chop up. Mix with vegetables and soup. Pour into 1 pie crust. Place second pie crust over the top and pinch edges together. Cut slit in top crust to allow vent. Bake until brown, about 15 to 20 minutes.

Penny Montefusco, a Soldiers' Angel in Orlando, Florida

Crab and Cream Cheese Wontons

1 pkg wonton wrappers 1 pkg lump crabmeat cream cheese	Mix crabmeat and cream cheese with spices and lemon juice to taste. I like some garlic, ginger, whatever. Follow instructions on wonton wrapper package to stuff wrappers with mixture. Cook wontons.

Faye Nettles, a Soldiers' Angel in Destin, Florida

Crab Quiche

6 - 7 oz crab meat 1 c shredded Swiss cheese 5 large eggs (to lower calories, use Egg Beaters and eliminate half-and-half) 1¼ c half-and-half ½ t black pepper ½ c sliced mushrooms 1 9-inch unbaked pie shell	Sprinkle cheese in pie shell. Beat eggs with half-and-half and mushrooms, and pour into shell. Sprinkle crab meat over pie. Bake 35 minutes at 375 until firm and knife, when inserted, comes out clean (about 50 minutes).

Faye Nettles, a Soldiers' Angel in Destin, Florida

Egg Salad, Destin Style

3 oz cream cheese, softened ¼ c mayonnaise ¾ t dill weed ½ t salt ½ t dry mustard 6 hard-cooked eggs, chopped ½ c sliced black olives ½ c chopped celery 2 T chopped onion	Thoroughly blend cream cheese, mayonnaise, and seasonings. Stir in remaining ingredients. After this, it's up to you. It's really wonderful in pita bread. Stores well in ice chest for picnics, too.

Faye Nettles, a Soldiers' Angel in Destin, Florida

Faye's Shrimp Brochette with Butter Sauce and Angel Hair Pasta

½ oz chopped shallots 2 oz white wine 2 oz white vinegar 1 stick butter, unsalted, at room temperature 1 can lump crabmeat salt and pepper to taste shrimp (s much as you like - headless and shelled) angel hair pasta, for serving	Place all ingredients in pan except butter, crab, and shrimp. Simmer slowly until liquid is almost evaporated. Remove from heat. Slowly incorporate butter. It should remain frothy and not broken. Oil and season shrimp (use a clove of garlic). Grill in frying pan 4 to 6 minutes. Add crab. Continue cooking until shrimp turns pinkish-white. Add butter sauce. Serve over angel hair pasta.

Faye Nettles, a Soldiers' Angel in Destin, Florida

Key Lime Pie

1¼ c graham cracker crumbs
2 T sugar
½ c butter (melted)
½ c key lime juice (freshly squeezed if possible; bottled key lime juice or regular lime juice can be substituted if necessary)
⅓ c sugar
⅛ t salt
2 T lime zest (coarsely grated)
2½ c heavy whipping cream
1 key lime

Heat oven to 350. In 9-inch pie plate, combine graham cracker crumbs and 2 tablespoons sugar; stir in butter until blended. Press mixture firmly and evenly over bottom and sides of pie plate; bake 10 minutes or until browned. Remove and cool completely on wire rack. In top of double boiler using wire whisk, beat egg yolks, lime juice, 1/3 cup sugar, and salt until well blended. Set over simmering water. Cook for about 5 minutes, stirring constantly until mixture is thick enough to coat back of metal spoon. Remove from heat. Stir in 1 tablespoon grated lime zest. Refrigerate mixture 45 minutes until cool. In large bowl with electric mixer at medium speed, beat cream until soft peaks form. Set 1 cup whipped cream aside for garnish. Fold cooled lime mixture into remaining cream. Spoon filling into pie crust. Slice lime and garnish with lime slices for each piece of pie.

Pam Andrews, a Soldiers' Angel in Port Orange, Florida

Minorcan Clam Chowder

⅓ lb salt pork
2 c chopped onion
2 c chopped celery
1 (12-oz) can chopped tomatoes
2 c diced potatoes
3 - 4 c diced clams (fresh or canned) and clam juice
2 stems fresh thyme
1 t salt and pepper
2 whole datil peppers

Cut salt pork in ¼-inch cubes, fry in cast iron skillet until crisp. Add onion and celery; sauté until onion is transparent. In cast iron pot, combine onion, celery, pork cubes, tomatoes, potatoes, 1 quart water, salt, pepper, thyme, and datil peppers. Cook on medium heat for 1 1/2 hours. Add clams and juice. Cook for additional 1/2 hour. For best flavor chill overnight. Reheat and eat.

Cherilyn Brown, a Soldiers' Angel in Lithia Springs, Georgia

Stuffed Pickles	
1 jar halved dill pickles 1 can tuna	Mix tuna to your liking. With a spoon, remove a portion of the inside of the pickle to make space for the stuffing. Turn pickles upside down on paper towels to drain. Stuff pickles with the tuna, just enough to fill the space so the pickle is still visible. You can cut each pickle into bite-sized pieces. Try stuffing with egg salad or ham salad.

Mardy Magyar, a Soldiers' Angel in Homosassa, Florida

Georgia

Bill's Short Ribs

2 T oil
2 lb short ribs
2 cloves garlic
2 ½ t salt
1 large onion, coarsely chopped
2 qt hot water
2 bullion beef cubes or 1 can double-
    strength beef broth (preferable)
2 stalks celery, cut into ½-inch pieces
4 carrots pared, cut into 1-inch pieces
4 zucchini trimmed, cut into ½-inch pieces
1 ear corn, quartered or ½ c whole kernel
    corn
	Brown meat all sides in oil. Mash garlic and salt together with side of knife and add to meat. Stir in onion and cook 3 minutes. Add water and broth and simmer 1 1/2 hours. Add vegetables (except corn) and cook 10 minutes. Add corn and cook 5 minutes. Serve warm with buttered French or Italian bread. Very good!

Gidget Barrett, a Soldiers' Angel in Temple, Georgia

Cinnamon Pecan Nuggets

3 c light brown sugar ⅛ t cinnamon 1 c evaporated milk ½ t vanilla extract 2 c chopped pecans 1 T butter	Combine the brown sugar, cinnamon, and evaporated milk in a medium saucepan. Heat over medium-high heat, stirring to dissolve the sugar. When the mixture begins to boil, connect a candy thermometer to the side of the pan. Heat to 232 F (112 C), or until a small amount of syrup dropped into cold water forms a soft ball that flattens when removed from the water and placed on a flat surface. Remove from the heat and use a sturdy wooden spoon to stir in vanilla. Add butter and pecans and continue to stir until thick and creamy. It will lose some of its shine. Drop spoonfuls onto waxed paper and allow to cool at room temperature until set. Store in an airtight container at room temperature.

Cherilyn Brown, a Soldiers' Angel in Lithia Springs, Georgia

Deep Dark Chocolate Cookies

¾ c butter or margarine, softened
¾ c sugar
½ c brown sugar, packed
1 t vanilla
2 eggs
1¾ c flour
½ c cocoa
¾ t baking soda
½ t baking powder
1 c semisweet chocolate chips
½ c nuts

Preheat oven to 375. In a large bowl, beat butter, sugars, and vanilla until light and fluffy. Add eggs. Beat well. In a small bowl, mix dry ingredients. Add to wet ingredients. Stir in chips and nuts. Drop by teaspoonfuls onto ungreased cookie sheets. Bake about 7 minutes. To make chocolate-mint blossoms, omit chips and nuts. When cookies are done, top with a mint kiss.

Marty Thompson, a Soldiers' Angel in Newnan, Georgia

Fudgey Brownies

1 (12-oz) bag chocolate chips
1 c margarine
4 eggs
2 c sugar
1 t vanilla
2 c flour
1 c chopped nuts (optional)

Preheat oven to 325. Combine chips and margarine; melt, stir well, and cool. Beat eggs, sugar, and vanilla with chocolate mixture. Add flour and nuts. Bake in a greased 9 x 12 inch pan for 35 minutes.

Marty Thompson, a Soldiers' Angel in Newnan, Georgia

Helen's Crab Quiche

1 (7½-oz) can crabmeat or 12 oz crabmeat 1 c cooked shrimp 8 oz grated Swiss cheese ⅓ c chopped celery ½ c chopped green onion ½ c mayonnaise 2 eggs, beaten 2 T flour ½ c dry white wine (optional) 1 t mustard 1 (10-inch) deep dish pie shell (partially baked so liquids won't get absorbed)	Preheat oven 350. Combine seafood, cheese, celery, and onions. Blend mayonnaise, mustard, and flour separately. Add seafood mixture and stir. Add 2 eggs, stir again; add wine; stir. Mixture should be thick. Pour into shell and bake until no longer raw in the middle about 55 minutes. Let rest before serving to firm up. Note: For those that need soft foods, sauté celery and onion first before filling to soften.

Gidget Barrett, a Soldiers' Angel in Temple, Georgia

Mom's American Goulash

2 lb beef chuck ½ c shortening 1 c sliced onion 1 clove garlic ¾ c catsup 2 T Worcestershire sauce 2 t paprika 2 t salt ½ t dry mustard dash red pepper 2 T flour ½ c water wide egg noodles, for serving	Brown meat in an electric skillet and fry to nice and caramelized. Add all the other ingredients (except noodles). Cook until beef is tender about 1 to 1 1/2 hours. Serve over egg noodles.

Gidget Barrett, a Soldiers' Angel in Temple, Georgia

Peach Pickles

1 gal peach halves, drained but juice saved 4 c peach juice 2 c sugar 4 cinnamon sticks 2 c white vinegar 3 – 4 whole cloves	Bring all ingredients, except peaches, to a boil. Add peaches. Simmer 5 to 6 minutes. Let peaches sit in liquid until cool. Pack into clean jars.

Albug, a Soldiers' Angel in Georgia

Swiss Steak

4 cube steaks 1 c flour 2 t seasoned salt 1 t garlic powder 2 T oil 2 onions 1 pkg brown gravy mix mashed potatoes, for serving	Put flour, salt, and garlic powder in a plastic bag. Add meat and shake until meat is coated. Heat oil in pan on medium heat. Fry steaks on both sides until brown. Remove from pan to plate. Fry onions until transparent. Remove to plate. Deglaze pan with water or beef broth. Add gravy mix, meat, and onions to pan. Add enough water to cover. Cook, covered, on medium low heat for 1 hour. Remove lid and cook 10 to 15 minutes or until gravy thickens. Serve over mashed potatoes.

Marty Thompson, a Soldiers' Angel in Newnan, Georgia

Hawai'i

Guri-guri

2 (12-oz) cans strawberry soda 1 (12-oz) can 7-Up 1 (14-oz) can sweetened condensed milk	Combine all ingredients in a large bowl and mix vigorously. Cover, and freeze for 1 to 2 hours. Remove from freezer and mix vigorously again. Repeat steps mixing and freezing at least twice. Transfer into individual cups (the cute itty bitty bathroom cups are perfect!) and freeze until firm. Remove from freezer and ENJOY! Note: You can also use different kinds of the 2-can soda to make different flavored guri-guri.

Jodi Fujimoto, a Soldiers' Angel in Lihue (Kaua'i), Hawai'i

Haupia

4 c coconut milk 2½ c water 1¼ c sugar 1 c cornstarch Optional crust: ½ c butter or margarine 3 T sugar 1 c flour ¼ c chopped nuts	Combine coconut milk and water. Stir until smooth. Add the sugar and cornstarch. Cook over low heat until thickened and shiny. If the haupia looks grainy, keep cooking the mixture because the fat in the coconut milk has not melted. Although this is not traditional, you can make a dough with 1/2 cup butter or margarine, 3 tablespoons of sugar, 1 cup of flour and 1/4 cup of chopped nuts. Press the dough into a pan and bake it for 15 minutes at 350. When the crust is cool, pour the haupia over the top, chill, and serve with whipped cream and sprinkle with toasted shredded coconut.

Deanna Peyatt, a Soldiers' Angel in Mililani (O'ahu), Hawai'i

Mango Bread, Maui Style

¾ c oil
2 c sugar
¼ c honey
3 eggs
1 t vanilla
2½ c flour white/wheat blend (¼ wheat; ¾ white)
½ t salt
3 t cinnamon
2 t baking soda
1 t baking powder
1 t lemon juice
2 c mango puree
½ c mashed apple bananas (about 2, but can use regular bananas)
1 c shredded coconut (optional, can add ½ to 1 t coconut extract instead)
1 c chopped walnuts or macadamia nuts

Preheat oven to 350. Grease 9 x 5 x 3 inch loaf pans or 4 small mini loaf pans and make cupcakes too! Cream with mixer or by hand, oil, sugar, honey; beat in eggs one at a time, in LARGE bowl. Stir in vanilla, set aside. Chop up mangos with the juice into a bowl, add lemon juice and banana, mash together or puree. (I like it mashed.) Sift dry ingredients together. Into the large bowl, stir in dry ingredients and mango/banana puree alternately. Lastly, stir in nuts and coconut. Bake at 350, 30 to 45 minutes, until tooth pick comes out clean.

Kathy Coombs, a Soldiers' Angel in Lahaina (Maui), Hawai'i

Mango Salsa

3 - 4 fresh mangoes
1 red onion
1 T chopped jalapeños
juice from 1 lime
1 T chopped cilantro

Peel and dice mangoes in a bowl. Add chopped red onion, the chopped jalapeños, and the cilantro. Top with the lime. This can be prepared ahead of time and marinate in the fridge. Great alone with corn chips or on top of grilled/baked chicken.

Deanna Peyatt, a Soldiers' Angel in Mililani (O'ahu), Hawai'i

Pineapple Upside Down Cake

6 T unsalted butter ½ c light brown sugar ½ c dark rum sliced canned pineapple in juice, drained maraschino cherries yellow cake mix or pineapple cake mix 1 c pineapple juice 3 eggs ⅓ c vegetable oil	In small saucepan, melt butter, brown sugar, and ¼ of rum over low heat. Do not use higher heat, as rum will flame! Pour into 13 x 9 baking dish. Cut pineapple slices in half and arrange, with cherries, on top of the mixture. Make cake, use juice instead of water. Add the remaining ¼ cup of rum to the batter and mix well. Pour batter evenly over the pineapple slices and smooth the top. Bake about 35 minutes, until a toothpick inserted in the center comes out clean. Let cool 5 minutes before inverting onto a serving platter. Don't wait too long, or it won't come out of the pan cleanly. Rum burns off…but can use rum flavor instead.

Kathy Coombs, a Soldiers' Angel in Lahaina (Maui), Hawai'i

Roast Loin of Pork with Bananas Baked in Orange Juice

1 (1½ - 2 lb) loin of pork 2 T finely chopped candied ginger ¼ c soy sauce 6 – 8 medium bananas, slightly under ripe is best 1 medium orange, peeled and chunked 2 T orange juice 2 T lemon juice ⅓ c sugar dash cinnamon dash nutmeg	Preheat oven to 325. With knife, make several slits in pork. Insert 1 tablespoon of the ginger. Combine rest of ginger and soy sauce. Place pork, fat side up, in roasting pan. Brush pork with part of ginger-soy mixture. For well-done roast, bake for 1¾ hours, brushing with ginger-soy mixture several times. Remove from oven and let sit 20 minutes before carving. For bananas, peel bananas and arrange in shallow baking dish. Add orange, orange juice, lemon juice, sugar, cinnamon, and nutmeg. Bake 25 to 30 minutes or until bananas are golden and tender. Serve hot with pork loin.

Myrna, a Soldiers' Angel in Hawai'i

Vacation Condo Pineapple Pie

1 (14-oz) can sweetened condensed milk 1 (8-oz) container frozen whipped topping, thawed 1 (20-oz) can crushed pineapple, well drained ⅔ c lemon juice 2 (9-inch) graham cracker crusts ½ c flaked coconut	In a large bowl, mix milk, whipped topping, drained pineapple, and lemon juice until blended and thick. Pour into 2 pie crusts, dividing evenly. Sprinkle each pie with ¼ cup coconut. Refrigerate until chilled. Bring to community barbeque at the pool and make new friends.

MaryAnn Foote, a Soldiers' Angel in Westlake Village, California

Idaho

Camp Bay Trout with Huckleberry Hash Browns

4 trout
1 c buttermilk
⅓ c flour
8 strips bacon
4 Idaho russet potatoes
1 Walla Walla Sweet onion
1 c fresh huckleberries
2 T bacon fat
salt and pepper to taste

Clean the trout, remove the fins but leave the heads and tails on. Dip in buttermilk and drain well. Mix flour with salt and pepper. Roll fish in mixture. Cook bacon in heavy skillet until half done. Reserve bacon fat in skillet to cook trout. Wrap each fish in 2 slices of semicooked bacon. Heat bacon fat in skillet. When hot, add trout and brown well on both sides. When cooked (approximately 3 minutes each side) remove to a hot serving platter and serve immediately. Peel and shred potatoes. Roughly chop onion. Mix potato and onion and season to taste. Heat oil in heavy skillet. Flatten mixture into bottom of skillet and sauté until golden brown and crispy. Flip mixture (hopefully) in 1 piece to cook other side. While second side browns, sprinkle top with huckleberries. When golden brown, remove from skillet and serve immediately with trout.

Karen Kemp, Camp Bay, Sandpoint, Idaho on the shores of Lake Pend d'Oreille

Chicken Enchiladas

2 chicken breasts
garlic to taste
2 T wine
½ c evaporated skim milk
1 T butter
1 T cornstarch
½ c nonfat cottage or ricotta cheese
½ c nonfat sour cream
3 T chopped onion
1 small can mushrooms, rinsed and
    drained
1 (4-oz) can green chilies, drained
4 tortillas
½ c grated mozzarella or Jack cheese

Cube and stir fry chicken breasts until no longer pink. Add garlic to taste and wine; stir fry 1 minute more. Shred chicken, if desired. Set aside. In blender, combine skim milk, butter, cornstarch, cottage cheese or ricotta, and sour cream. Blend. Reserve 1/2 cup mixture. Add remaining mixture to shredded chicken, and then add onion, mushrooms, and green chilies. Stir and spoon into 4 tortillas. Place seam side down in glass baking dish, top with reserved 1/2 cup mixture and grated cheese. Bake 30 minutes at 350 or until hot and bubbly, or microwave for 6 minutes or until mixture is hot and cheese is melted.

Mary Nasfell, a Soldiers' Angel in Boise, Idaho

Curly Chicken Pasta

2 chicken breasts garlic to taste 2 T wine 1 (8-oz) package rotini 1½ T white wine vinegar (or other vinegar) 3 T sesame oil (or vegetable oil) 3 T blended plum chutney (or plum jam) 3 T soy sauce cayenne or hot sauce ½ c chopped fresh spinach 2 T sesame seeds 6 green onions chopped 1 T chopped parsley	Cube and stir fry chicken until no longer pink. Add garlic to taste and wine. Stir fry 1 minute and set aside. Cook pasta and drain. In a large bowl, combine vinegar, sesame oil, chutney, soy sauce, and a small amount of cayenne or hot sauce. Combine chicken and pasta. Pour sauce over. Add rest of ingredients. Mix and serve. May be served warm or chilled and served as a salad.

Mary Nasfell, a Soldiers' Angel in Boise, Idaho

Gremlin Bars

1 box German chocolate cake mix ⅔ c evaporated milk ¾ c margarine, melted 1½ c chopped nuts 1 pkg (about 50) caramels 1 (6-oz) pkg chocolate chips	Mix cake mix, 1/3 cup milk, margarine, and 1 cup chopped nuts. Melt caramels in other 1/3 cup milk. Press 1/2 of cake mixture into greased and floured 9 x 13 inch pan, bake at 350 for 8 minutes. Remove from oven, sprinkle chocolate chips over crust, pour melted caramel mixture over, drop spoonfuls of remaining batter over caramel mixture, sprinkle with 1/2 cup chopped nuts. Bake 350° for 18 to 20 minutes. Cool in pan. Refrigerate to set up caramel.

Mary Nasfell, a Soldiers' Angel in Boise, Idaho

Pumpkin Muffins	
1½ c whole wheat flour 3 t baking powder 2 t cinnamon ¼ t ginger ¼ t nutmeg 1 c canned pumpkin ½ c orange juice ¼ c brown sugar ¼ c molasses ¼ c applesauce 1 c raisins	Mix all ingredients only until moistened. Spray or oil 12 muffin tins. Spoon in batter. Bake at 375 for 20 minutes.

Mary Nasfell, a Soldiers' Angel in Boise, Idaho

Illinois

Chicken Boudine

2 c cooked egg noodles 2 (10 ¾-oz) cans cream of mushroom soup ½ c chicken broth ¼ c dry sherry 4 c chopped cooked chicken 3 c grated sharp cheese, your choice, divided 1 (2¼-oz) pkg slivered almonds, toasted ¼ c drained, chopped pimentos 1 (4-oz) can sliced mushrooms, drained salt and pepper	Preheat oven to 350. In a large bowl, toss together the noodles, soup, broth, and sherry. Add the chicken, 2 cups of the cheese, the almonds, pimento, mushrooms, and salt and pepper, to taste, and toss gently to combine. Transfer the mixture to a greased 13 x 9 x 2-inch casserole and top with the remaining cup of cheese. Bake for 30 minutes, or until bubbly.

Tonya, a Soldiers' Angel in Illinois

Chicken Quesadillas

¼ c mayonnaise 2 t minced jalapeños, slices 2 t jalapeño juice, from minced jalapeños ¾ t sugar ½ t cumin ½ t paprika ⅛ t cayenne pepper ⅛ t garlic powder 1 dash salt 4 flour tortillas 4 chicken tenderloins 1 c shredded Cheddar cheese 1 c shredded Fiesta cheese	Combine mayonnaise, jalapeños and juice, sugar, and spices and stir until smooth. Grill chicken in vegetable oil and cut into thin slices. Preheat skillet over medium heat. One at a time, lay tortilla into hot skillet and sprinkle with 1/4 cup of shredded Cheddar cheese. Arrange about 1/4 cup chicken slices over tortilla on the same half covered with cheese. Sprinkle Fiesta cheese over chicken. On the empty side, spread about one tablespoon of sauce. Fold over, and press gently with spatula. Cook until cheese is melted and slice each into 4 pieces.

Dawn Claro, a Soldiers' Angel in Benld, Illinois

Ham and Potato Soup

3½ c peeled and diced potatoes ⅓ c finely chopped onion ¾ c diced cooked ham 3¼ c water 2 T chicken bouillon granules ½ t salt, or to taste 1 t ground white or black pepper, or to taste 5 T butter 5 T all-purpose flour 2 c milk	Combine the potatoes, onion, ham, and water in a stockpot. Bring to a boil, then cook over medium heat until potatoes are tender, about 10 to 15 minutes. Stir in the chicken bouillon, salt, and pepper. In a separate saucepan, melt butter over medium-low heat. Whisk in flour with a fork, and cook, stirring constantly until thick, about 1 minute. Slowly stir in milk as not to allow lumps to form until all of the milk has been added. Continue stirring over medium-low heat until thick, 4 to 5 minutes. Stir the milk mixture into the stockpot, and cook soup until heated through. Serve immediately.

Dawn Claro, a Soldiers' Angel in Benld, Illinois

Illinois Winter Vegetable Soup

1½ lb ground round 1 (15-oz) can kidney beans ½ c diced onion 2 cloves garlic 1 c celery 1½ t basil 1 c carrots 2 c water 5 t beef bouillon 1½ t oregano 2 (16-oz) cans tomatoes 4 t black pepper 1 (15-oz) can tomato sauce ½ c frozen corn ½ bag of Kluski noodles 2 c cabbage 1 can French cut green beans	Mix beef, beans, onions, garlic, celery, basil, carrots, water, bouillon, oregano, tomatoes, black pepper, and tomato sauce, and simmer 45 minutes. Next, add corn, noodles, cabbage, and green beans, and simmer another 30 minutes. This will warm you up.

Pat Short, a Soldiers' Angel in Gilman, Illinois

Midwestern Hash Browns

3 c finely shredded raw potatoes 1 T grated onion 1 T chopped parsley ½ t salt ¼ t black pepper 3 T butter, bacon drippings, or other fat ¼ c cream	Combine all the ingredients, except the fat. Put the fat into a heated heavy 9-inch fry pan. Spread potato mixture over the bottom of the pan and, with a spatula press it down to form a cake. Sauté slowly, shaking the potatoes from time to time to keep from sticking. When bottom is brown, cut potato layer in half and turn each with 2 spatulas. Pour ¼ cup cream over the potatoes. Brown the second side and serve immediately.

Vicky Fisher, a Soldiers' Angel in Carbondale, Illinois

Nick's Favorite Welcome Home Casserole

3 bags frozen chopped broccoli 1 small box Ritz Crackers (MUST use this brand) 1 stick butter 1 large pkg Velveeta cheese singles salt and pepper to taste	Cook broccoli in just enough water to cover. Sprinkle in salt and pepper and a pat of butter. Cook until tender but still bright green. Drain almost all the water out, leaving only about 1 cup in bottom of the pan to moisten the casserole. Butter the bottom and sides of a 9 x 13 inch baking pan. Crush 3 sleeves of cracker until fine crumbs. Sprinkle over bottom of baking pan. Layer the cooked broccoli on top of the crackers. Pour cooking water on top. Unwrap cheese and place in uniform order on top of broccoli. Bake at 325 for about 15 minutes or until cheese is melted. Cut into 12 squares. I always serve this with a big country ham and all the fixings when my son comes home on leave.

Debi L McCrillis, a Soldiers' Angel in Machesney Park, Illinois

Only Way to Eat Green Beans

¼ lb sliced bacon 3 (14½-oz) cans green beans, with liquid ¼ yellow onion 1 t granulated sugar ½ t salt ½ t fresh ground black pepper	In a 2-quart saucepan over medium heat, cook bacon until lightly brown but not crisp. When bacon has browned, add green beans. Add salt, sugar, and pepper and mix well. Place onion on top of green beans. Cover saucepan with a lid and bring to a light boil. Turn heat down to low and simmer beans for 45 minutes.

Dawn Claro, a Soldiers' Angel in Benld, Illinois

Party Taco Salad

2 lb ground beef 2 pkg taco seasoning mix 16 oz Cheddar cheese, shredded 1 red onion, chopped 1 yellow onion, chopped 2 heads iceberg lettuce, chopped 4 tomatoes, chopped 2 avocados, chopped 2 green peppers, chopped 1 can black olives, chopped 1 large bag nacho chips, crumbled 1 (8-oz) bottle Catalina salad dressing	Brown ground beef with chopped yellow onion. Add 1 package taco seasoning and water according to package directions. Set aside to cool completely. In a large bowl mix chopped lettuce, tomato, cheese, avocado, red onion, peppers, olives, and second package of taco seasoning. Add cooled beef mixture. Just before serving, toss with the dressing. The last step is to mix in 3/4 of the package of crushed nacho chips, leaving the rest on the side for people who want extra (they get soggy if you do them too early).

Tonya, a Soldiers' Angel in Illinois

Pepsi Pork Roast

Boston butt or any other kind of pork roast you have on hand 1 (12-oz) can Pepsi 1 (10¾-oz) can cream of mushroom soup ½ (1¼-oz) pkg onion soup mix	Place roast in crock pot. Mix soup mix with soup. Add Pepsi to soup mixture and pour over roast. Cook on high for 4 to 5 hours. When done, remove roast and thicken juices with cornstarch for gravy.

Dawn Claro, a Soldiers' Angel in Benld, Illinois

Pork and Bean Bread

1 c raisins (optional) 1 c boiling water (if using raisins) 3 eggs 1 c oil 2 c sugar 1 (16-oz) can pork and beans (mashed) 3 c flour 1 t cinnamon ½ t baking powder 1 t baking soda ½ t salt 1 t vanilla 1 c chopped nuts (optional)	Heat oven to 325. Generously grease 3 loaf pans. Stir raisins into boiling water; set aside. Beat eggs, oil, sugar, and pork and beans until beans are broken. Add flour, cinnamon, baking powder, baking soda and salt. Stir in vanilla and nuts. Drain raisins and add them to mixture, stir well. Pour batter into prepared pans and bake for 50 to 60 minutes.

Pat Short, a Soldiers' Angel in Gilman, Illinois

Wilted Salad Pepper Steak

1½ lb round steak flour 4 T fat 3 medium green peppers, chopped 2 medium onions 2 t Worcestershire sauce 2½ c water salt and pepper to taste	Cut steak into pieces about 2 x 3 inches. Roll in flour and brown in fat. Add peppers, onions, Worcestershire sauce, and half the water. Season well, cover, and simmer over a low flame until tender, about 1½ hours. Add the remaining water from time to time during the cooking. Adjust seasoning to taste.

Vicky Fisher, a Soldiers' Angel in Carbondale, Illinois

'Ziploc' Omelet

2 eggs per person cheese, ham, onion, green pepper, tomatoes, salsa, etc	Have guests/family write their name on a quart-size Ziploc freezer bag using a permanent marker. Crack 2 eggs into each bag and shake to combine. Each person adds ingredients of choice to the bag; shake to combine. Squeeze air from bag and zip up. Place bags into rolling, boiling water for exactly 13 minutes. You can cook 6 to 8 omelets in a large pot all at once. Open the bag and the omelet will roll out. Serve with fresh fruit and coffee cake. Great for camping, too. You can prepare bags the night before, refrigerate, and cook the next morning. No waiting for an omelet when there is a crowd!

Pat Short, a Soldiers' Angel in Gilman, Illinois

Indiana

Brain Sandwiches

1 lb pork brains 1 large egg, beaten ½ c flour ½ t baking powder vegetable oil milk salt and pepper to taste large hamburger buns, for serving	For the daring… Soak brains in salt water approximately 1 hour. Rinse, cover with clear water, remove membranes and discard; check for bone chips! Drain and gently stir in other ingredients with a spoon. Don't stir too hard or brains will turn to mush! (Batter needs to be of medium thickness...if too thin, add small amounts of flour; if too thick, add small amounts of milk.) Spoon into 1/2 inch oil heated in iron skillet. (Make a patty.) Fry approximately 10 minutes each side for a 1/2 thick patty, longer if patty is thicker. Drain and pat with paper towels to remove oil, serve on toasted bun! Most popular condiments are pickle, onion, and mustard. These originally were made with calf brains, but Mad Cow disease makes them too risky!

Kathy Santiago, a Soldiers' Angel in Indiana

Chess Cake

1 (18.25-oz) box yellow cake mix 4 eggs 1 c butter, melted (divided) 1 (8-oz) pkg cream cheese, softened 4 c confectioners' sugar	Preheat oven to 325. Grease and flour a 9 x 13 inch pan. In a large bowl, mix cake mix, 2 eggs, and 1/2 cup melted butter. Put into prepared pan. In another bowl, beat cream cheese until smooth. Blend in 1/2 cup melted butter and 2 eggs. Gradually beat in the confectioner's sugar. Pour over the crust mixture already in the pan. Bake for 1 hour. Cool. I have also used spice cake, chocolate, lemon, and pumpkin cake mixes!!!

LoriAnn Kocialski, a Soldiers' Angel in Indianapolis, Indiana

Coke Cake

1 c butter 2 c flour 1¾ c sugar 3 t cocoa 1 t baking soda 1 t vanilla 2 eggs ½ c buttermilk 1 c (any brand) canned cola 1½ c miniature marshmallows Frosting: ½ c butter 3 T cocoa ⅓ c cola 4 c powdered sugar	Combine softened butter, flour, sugar, cocoa, baking soda, vanilla, eggs, and buttermilk. Add cola, blend well and stir in marshmallows by hand. Pour into a greased pan and bake at 350 for 30 to 40 minutes. Cool for 30 minutes before frosting. Toast 1/2 cup almonds in oven and stir into frosting, if desired. It adds a great flavor. This cake is said to be a favorite of Dave Letterman.

LoriAnn Kocialski, a Soldiers' Angel in Indianapolis, Indiana

Fried Pork Tenderloin Sandwich

1 pork tenderloin (cut into ¾ inch slices)
saltine crackers, made into meal (use a
    blender or processor)
1 c water
1 T (I use Maggi brand chicken and tomato
    but any brand or flavor will do. Three of
    the cube variety work well)
oil (for frying)
4 hamburger buns, for serving
condiments, for serving
	Pound pork slices until each is about 1/4 inch thick. Place the cracker meal in a dish (aluminum pie pans work great). In a second dish, pour in the water and stir in the bouillon. Dip each slice in the bouillon water and then in the cracker meal. Coat well. Deep fry in a fry daddy or deep fryer at 375 until golden brown. (Pan frying works equally well). Drain. Serve on a hamburger bun with your choice of condiments.

LoriAnn Kocialski, a Soldiers' Angel in Indianapolis, Indiana

Hoosier Sugar Cream Pie

1⅓ c sugar
½ c all-purpose flour, unsifted
1 c whipping cream
¾ c milk
1 (9-inch) unbaked pie shell
2 T butter, cut into small pieces
pinch nutmeg

Preheat oven to 450 (if using a glass baking dish, lower oven temperature by 25 degrees). Combine sugar, flour, cream, and milk in a mixing bowl. Pour into pie shell. Dot butter bits all around top of pie. Sprinkle with nutmeg. Bake for approximately 10 minutes, and then reduce the heat to 350 and cook for approximately 30 more minutes. Cool to room temperature and then refrigerate until chilled. Serve chilled.

Heather Davis, a Soldiers' Angel in Elnora, Indiana

Indiana State Pie – Sugar Cream Pie

pastry for 9-inch one-crust pie
¾ c granulated pure cane sugar
5 T all-purpose flour
2½ c heavy whipping cream, room
    temperature
1 t pure vanilla extract
whole nutmeg

Preheat oven to 450 and prepare pie pastry. Place sugar and flour in the unbaked pie shell. Add cream and mix well using your fingers to slowly mix the dry and liquid ingredients (prevent the cream from whipping). Add vanilla extract to the mixture and continue stirring with your fingers. Grate nutmeg over the top. Bake 10 minutes; reduce heat to 350 and continue baking approximately 1 hour. Remove from oven. NOTE: Do not over bake. The pie may appear runny but usually sets as it cools. Overbaking seems to break down the sugar and the pie never solidifies. If the pie doesn't set, get out some spoons and enjoy it anyway. Although you may refrigerate the pie, it usually isn't necessary to get it to set.

LoriAnn Kocialski, a Soldiers' Angel in Indianapolis, Indiana

Persimmon Cookies

1 c sugar ¾ c butter 2 eggs 1 c persimmon pulp 1 t baking powder 1 t vanilla 1 t cinnamon ½ t nutmeg ½ t salt 2 c flour ½ c raisins ½ c nuts	Dissolve soda in the pulp. Cream sugar and butter. Add vanilla and beaten eggs. Sift dry ingredients. Add with pulp. Then add raisins and nuts. Drop cookies by teaspoon on ungreased cookie sheet. Bake until puffed and golden brown at 350.

Heather Davis, a Soldiers' Angel in Elnora, Indiana

Persimmon Pudding

1 stick butter, melted 2 c persimmon pulp 1½ c sugar 1½ c milk (regular milk or canned) 3 eggs 2 c flour 1 medium sweet potato, grated 1 c coconut (optional) 1 t baking soda 1 t allspice 1 t cloves 1 t vanilla extract	Bake in 300 oven for 1 hour or until done. A broiler pan is a nice size to bake it in.

LoriAnn Kocialski, a Soldiers' Angel in Indianapolis, Indiana

Rhubarb Crunch

1 c sugar 1 c water 2 T cornstarch 1 t vanilla 1 c flour 1 c oatmeal 1 c brown sugar ½ c melted butter 1 t cinnamon 4 c chopped rhubarb	Mix 1 cup sugar, water, and cornstarch. Cook and set aside. Mix flour, oatmeal, brown sugar, butter, and cinnamon until crumbly. Put 1/2 inch of crunch in bottom of a 9 X 9 pan. Add rhubarb. Pour in cooked mixture. Put rest of crunch on top. Bake for 1 hour at 350.

Heather Davis, a Soldiers' Angel in Elnora, Indiana

Iowa

Cole Slaw

1 large head cabbage 1 green pepper 1 onion 1 c sour cream 1 c mayonnaise 3 T vinegar 1 t celery seed 1 c (or less) sugar salt and pepper to taste	Shred cabbage, green pepper, and onion; place in a large bowl. In a medium bowl, combine dressing ingredients; blend well. Pour dressing over vegetables and mix well.

Jean, a Soldiers' Angel in New Mexico

Pork Chops and Corn Dressing

4 pork chops ½ t salt ½ t pepper 3 T water 6 slices bread 1 can cream-style corn 1 small onion, chopped ¼ c melted margarine	Season chops with salt and pepper and brown them. Place in baking dish. Add water. Mix cubed bread, corn, onion, and margarine. Top each chop with some dressing or slit the edge (if using thick Iowa chops) and put dressing there. Bake at 350 for 45 minutes. Yummy!

orengeblossoms4me, a Soldiers' Angel in Grinnell, Iowa

Pork Chop 'N Potato Bake

6 pork chops vegetable oil seasoning salt 1 can (10.75-oz) condensed cream of celery soup ½ c milk ½ c sour cream ¼ t pepper 1 (24-oz) pkg frozen hash browns 1 c shredded Cheddar cheese 1 can French fried onions	Heat oven to 350. Brown pork chops in lightly greased skillet. Sprinkle with seasoning salt; set aside. Combine soup, milk, sour cream, pepper, and 1/2 teaspoon seasoning salt. Stir in potatoes, 1/2 cup cheese and 1/2 can French fried onions. Spoon mixture into 13 x 9 x 2-inch pan. Arrange pork chops over potatoes. Bake, covered, for 40 minutes. Top with remaining cheese and onions; bake, uncovered, 5 minutes longer.

Jean, a Soldiers' Angel in New Mexico

Kansas

Banana Sunflower Seed Cookies

1½ c all-purpose flour 1 t baking soda 2 very ripe medium bananas, peeled and mashed ½ c butter, at room temperature ½ c granulated white sugar ½ c shelled sunflower seeds ½ c miniature chocolate chips or dried fruit	Whisk together flour and baking soda in a small bowl. Set aside. In a large bowl, beat bananas, butter, and sugar on medium speed until thoroughly combined. Add flour mixture half at a time, beating to incorporate. Fold in sunflower seeds and chocolate chips. Refrigerate cookie dough for 45 minutes to 1 hour. (Cold dough helps keep the cookies from spreading) Preheat oven to 350. Line baking sheets with Silpats or parchment paper. Scoop about 1 teaspoonful of cookie dough for each cookie and place 2 inches apart on prepared baking sheets. Bake 12 to 15 minutes until edges are lightly golden.

Vanessa Bishop, a Soldiers' Angel in Texas

Brownies for Our Troops

2 sq (1 oz each) unsweetened chocolate ⅓ c butter-flavored shortening 2 eggs ½ t vanilla ¾ c flour ½ t baking powder ½ t salt ½ c chopped nuts (optional) chocolate chips (optional) tub of chocolate frosting (melted)	Heat chocolate and shortening in medium saucepan over low heat until melted and remove from heat. Mix in sugar, eggs, and vanilla. Stir in remaining ingredients. Spread in 8 x 8 x 2 greased disposable baking pan. Bake 350 for 30 to 35 minutes or until brownies begin to pull away from sides of pan. Cool. Spread melted frosting on brownies and put in freezer for several minutes to set. (This makes cutting easier.) Cut with plastic knife into squares and decorate with colored sprinkles and candies or whatever the season may be. Put the disposable lid on the pan, seal completely with tape, wrap in bubble wrap, and it is ready to send overseas.

Jo Johnson, a Soldiers' Angel in Olathe, Kansas, and 2 Blue Star Mom

Cheesy Potato Casserole

32-oz pkg shredded hash browns, thawed ⅓ c plus ½ c melted butter ½ c chopped onion (optional) 1 can cream of chicken soup 1 can cheddar cheese soup 1 pt sour cream 2 c grated cheese salt and pepper to taste 2 c crushed corn flakes	Preheat oven to 350. Mix ⅓ cup butter, soups, sour cream, and cheese in large mixing bowl. Add hash browns and mix thoroughly. Spread into greased 9 x 13 baking dish. Mix crushed corn flakes and ½ cup melted butter and sprinkle over potatoes. Bake uncovered for 1 hour.

Jo Johnson, a Soldiers' Angel in Olathe, Kansas, and 2 Blue Star Mom

Chicken Enchiladas

4 skinless, boneless chicken breast halves 1 onion, chopped ½ pt sour cream 1 c shredded Cheddar cheese 1 T dried parsley ½ t dried oregano ½ t ground black pepper ½ t salt (optional) 1 (8-oz) can tomato sauce 1 T chili powder (Williams is the best) ⅓ c chopped green bell pepper 1 clove garlic, minced 8 (10-inch) flour tortillas 1 (12-oz) jar taco sauce	Preheat oven to 350. In a medium, nonstick skillet over medium heat, prepare the chicken in chicken broth until it is no longer pink. Drain liquid; shred or cube the chicken and return it to the skillet. Sauté onion, green peppers, and garlic until soft. Mix together sour cream, Cheddar cheese, parsley, oregano, and ground black pepper. Heat until cheese melts. Stir in salt, tomato sauce, chili powder, the sautéed onion, green peppers, and garlic. Roll even amounts of the mixture in the tortillas. Arrange in a 9 x 13-inch baking dish. Cover with taco sauce and ¾ cup Cheddar cheese. Bake uncovered in the preheated oven 20 minutes. Cool 10 minutes before serving. Suggestions: Instead of the green pepper use green chilies, more chili powder, and a few dashes of ground cayenne pepper to spice it up. For a rich and creamy flavor, try adding a few tablespoons of cream cheese, some Monterey Jack and refried beans. Instead of using chicken all the time to change it up, use about 1½ lb of ground beef or ground turkey

Ellen Garcia, a Soldiers' Angel in Shawnee, Kansas

Chocolate Chip Cookies

½ c oatmeal 2¼ c flour 1½ t baking soda ½ t salt ¼ t cinnamon 1 c butter, softened ¾ c firmly packed brown sugar ¾ c sugar 2 t vanilla 1 t lemon juice 2 eggs 3 c semisweet chocolate chips	Preheat oven to 350. Put oatmeal in blender or food processor and process until firmly ground. Combine ground oats, flour, baking soda, salt, and cinnamon in mixing bowl. In another bowl, cream butter, sugars, vanilla, and lemon juice using an electric mixer. Add eggs and beat until fluffy. Stir the flour mixture into the egg mixture, blending well. Add chocolate chips and mix well. Roll into balls (about 1/4 cup each) and place on ungreased baking sheets 2 1/2 inches apart. Flatten each cookie with the back of a teaspoon just a bit. Bake 16 to 18 minutes or until lightly browned. Transfer to wire rack to cool completely. These are ready to wrap cookies back-to-back with plastic wrap, wrap in bubble wrap, and send overseas. Note: Can substitute chocolate chips for raisins or butterscotch chips. The lemon juice keeps the cookies moist and chewy.

Jo Johnson, a Soldiers' Angel in Olathe, Kansas, and 2 Blue Star Mom

Kansas Dirt

1 large pkg chocolate sandwich cookies (ie, Oreos) ½ c butter, softened 1 large carton frozen whipped topping, thawed 3 c chilled milk 1 t vanilla 1 (8-oz) pkg cream cheese 1 c powdered sugar 2 (3½ oz) pkg instant chocolate pudding	Crush cookies and press half in bottom of 9 x 13 baking dish. Mix cream cheese and butter until smooth. Mix in powdered sugar, and then fold in whipped topping. Beat together: pudding mixes, milk, and vanilla. Fold in with cream cheese mixture and spread over cookie crust. Sprinkle the rest of cookie crumbs over top of pudding mixture. Chill and serve. Note: You can use your imagination with this recipe. It is fun to put this into clean clay flower pots and have gummy worms on top and hanging over the sides of the flower pots.

Jo Johnson, a Soldiers' Angel in Olathe, Kansas, and 2 Blue Star Mom

Kansas Tomato Sandwich

2 slices white bread 1 medium tomato, thickly sliced 1 slice white American cheese 2 t butter or margarine 1 lettuce leaf (optional) salt and pepper to taste	Toast the bread slices to your desired darkness. When done, spread lightly with butter or margarine. Place a slice of tomato on the buttered side of one slice, and top with a slice of cheese. Season to taste with salt and pepper and place a slice of lettuce on if desired. Top with the remaining slice of bread. Enjoy!

Pam Krider, a Soldiers' Angel in Grainfield, Kansas

Penne Pasta Bake

1 (12-oz) pkg penne pasta 1 lb ground beef or sausage 1 c chopped onion 1 (15-oz) can Italian-style tomato sauce 1 (15-oz) can diced tomatoes with Italian herbs 1 (6-oz) can Italian paste with roasted garlic ½ c water 4 c shredded mozzarella cheese	Preheat oven to 350. Cook pasta according to package directions; drain. Cook meat and onion in large skillet over medium to high heat for 5 minutes; drain. Stir in tomato sauce, undrained tomatoes, tomato paste, and water. Cook, stirring occasionally, for about 10 minutes. Layer half pasta, half sauce, and half cheese in 9 x 13 baking dish, and repeat. Cover and bake in preheated oven for 20 minutes.

Jo Johnson, a Soldiers' Angel in Olathe, Kansas, and 2 Blue Star Mom

Sunflower Chicken Stir-Fry

2 T sesame oil
2 t minced fresh ginger
½ t garlic powder
1 lb chicken breasts, cut into bite-size
    pieces
4 c cold cooked rice
1 c chopped green onion
1 c chopped celery
1 c chopped carrots
½ c shelled sunflower seeds
¼ c soy sauce, divided
1 egg beaten with 1 t water

Whisk together sesame oil, ginger, and garlic powder. Add to chicken and toss to coat. Heat electric skillet or wok to 375. When hot, add chicken and sear on both sides. Add green onions, celery, carrots, sunflower seeds, and half of the soy sauce. Stir-fry until heated, then add egg, continuing to stir-fry. When egg has cooked, add the rice and remaining soy sauce. Stir-fry on high until rice is hot.

Vanessa Bishop, a Soldiers' Angel in Texas

Trash Snack Mix

1 c toasted oat cereal
1 c old-fashioned rolled oats
½ c shredded coconut
½ c whole unsalted almonds
½ c wheat germ
½ c shelled unsalted sunflower seeds
½ c raisins
½ c honey
¼ c light corn syrup
¼ c vegetable oil
1 t vanilla extract
1 t almond extract

Preheat oven to 325. In a large bowl, stir together cereal, rolled oats, coconut, almonds, wheat germ, sunflower seeds, and raisins. In a medium bowl, use medium speed of an electric mixer to beat honey, corn syrup, oil, vanilla, and almond extract until well blended. Pour honey mixture over dry ingredients, stirring until well coated. Spread evenly on a greased baking sheet. Bake 20 to 25 minutes or until brown. Cool completely in pan. Break into pieces. Store snacks in an airtight container. Yield: about 5-1/2 cups snack mix

Vanessa Bishop, a Soldiers' Angel in Texas

Kentucky

Butter Pecan Gooey Cake

3 eggs 1 stick butter, melted 1 box cake mix (I used butter pecan) 2 c powdered sugar 1 (8-oz) pkg cream cheese	Preheat oven to 350. Butter or spray oil a 9 x 13 inch pan. Mix 1 egg, melted butter, and cake mix. Pat/spread the mixture on the bottom of pan (mixture will be thick). Mix 2 eggs, sugar, and cream cheese on low till blended. Pour on top of bottom mixture (should be a little "soupy"). Bake at 350 for 30 to 35 minutes (until the sides pull from the pan). Sprinkle with powdered sugar. Serve warm, but it is also good cold!

Terri A Connor, a Soldiers' Angel in Burlington, Kentucky

Candied Cucumber Rings

5 large yellow cucumbers, (peeled, seeded, and cut into rings) 2 c lime (note, not the fruit!) 4 c vinegar 1 bottle red food coloring 10 c sugar 8 sticks cinnamon 2 pkg cinnamon candies (ie, Red Hots)	Combine cucumber and lime with 2 gallons water. Let stand for 24 hours. Drain and then rinse in clear water. Place cucumbers, red food coloring, 1 cup vinegar, and just enough water to cover the cucumbers. Let stand 3 hours, then drain and set aside. Combine 3 cups vinegar, 2 cups water, sugar, red hot candies, and cinnamon sticks. Bring to boil, stirring until sugar is dissolved. Pour over cucumbers. Let stand for 24 hours. Repeat process for 1 more day, then heat syrup and cucumbers. Pack into hot sterilized jars, covering cucumbers with syrup. Cover with sterilized lids and bands, screwing bands tight.

Darla Davidson, a Soldiers' Angel in Hardin, Kentucky

Egg Pie

4 eggs 3 c milk 1 T flour ½ c sugar 1 t nutmeg ¼ t cinnamon unbaked pie shell	Mix sugar and eggs until sugar is dissolved and add flour. Mix well. Add milk. Pour in unbaked pie shell. Sprinkle nutmeg and cinnamon on top. Bake at 425 until firm (knife stuck in the middle of the pie will come out clean).

Darla Davidson, a Soldiers' Angel in Hardin, Kentucky

Hot Dog Soup

1 pkg hot dogs, sliced salt and pepper to taste 1 small onion, chopped celery, chopped; as much as you like 6 beef bouillon cubes 4 T bacon grease macaroni (optional)	Put all ingredients in a 2-qt cooking pot. Add enough water to cover all ingredients. Bring to boil, then reduce heat and simmer until onions and celery are tender.

Darla Davidson, a Soldiers' Angel in Hardin, Kentucky

Kentucky Derby Pie

1 c sugar ½ c flour 2 eggs, beaten 1 c English walnuts 1 c chocolate chips 1 t pure vanilla extract ½ c melted butter 1 ready-made pie crust	Mix flour and sugar. Add eggs, then butter. Add nuts, chocolate chips, and vanilla extract. Mix thoroughly. Pour mixture into an unbaked pie shell. Bake in a preheated 350 oven for 35 to 45 minutes. Test with tooth pick; pie should be chewy but not runny. Bake longer, if necessary. I will state it is extremely rich!

Rhonda6747, a Soldiers' Angel in Kentucky

Kentucky Hot Brown

2 T butter, melted ¼ c flour 2 c milk ¼ t salt ½ t Worcestershire sauce 1 c grated sharp cheese 1 lb sliced turkey 8 slices bacon, cooked 4 slices tomato 8 slices toast 4 oz Parmesan cheese	Melt butter in saucepan, add flour, stir well. Add milk, cheeses, and seasonings. Cook stirring constantly until thick. Arrange turkey on toast and cover with cheese sauce. Place sandwiches under broiler until sauce begins to bubble. Garnish with crumbled bacon and tomato slices. Sprinkle with Parmesan cheese and serve immediately.

KanK, a Soldiers' Angel in Kentucky

Make Your Own Crust Coconut Pie

4 eggs, well beaten ½ c flour 1¾ c sugar ½ stick butter at room temperature 1 t vanilla 2 c milk 1 (6- or 7-oz) can coconut	Mix all ingredients well. Pour into two 9-inch baking pans. Bake at 350 for 30 minutes.

Darla Davidson, a Soldiers' Angel in Hardin, Kentucky

Victorian Vinegar Cookies

½ c butter ½ c margarine ¾ c sugar 1 T white vinegar 1 t vanilla 1¼ c flour ½ t baking soda 1 t salt 1 c finely chopped nuts (I usually use pecans, but walnuts are also good)	Cream butter, margarine, and sugar. Add white vinegar and vanilla. Sift flour, baking soda, and salt and blend into creamed mixture. Add nuts. Use small cookie scoop, these spread. Bake at 300 for 30 minutes.

Karen Sparks, a Soldiers' Angel in Kentucky

Louisiana

Buttermilk Pralines

2 c sugar 1 t baking soda 1 c buttermilk pinch salt 2 T butter 1 t vanilla 2¼ c pecans	Cook sugar, soda, buttermilk, and salt in large heavy saucepan until a soft ball forms in cold water. Remove from heat and cool. Add butter, vanilla, and pecans. Beat until stiff and creamy. Drop by spoonfuls on waxed paper. Enjoy!

Sue Abshire, a Soldiers' Angel in Baton Rouge, Louisiana

Buttermilk Pie

4 egg yolks 1½ c sugar ½ c melted butter 3 T flour 1½ c buttermilk 1 t vanilla 1 unbaked pie shell	Cream together egg yolks, sugar, butter, and flour. Add buttermilk and vanilla. Pour into unbaked pie shell. Place in oven preheated to 500. Reduce heat to 300. Bake until filling is set and pie is desired shade of golden brown. (Approximate time unknown.) Baking time depends on your oven.

Lisa0809, a Soldiers' Angel in Louisiana

Crawfish Etouffeé

3 large onions, chopped 1½ sticks butter 2 lb crawfish tails, cleaned crawfish fat salt and red pepper to taste parsley, finely chopped green onion tops only, finely chopped rice, for serving	Sauté onions in butter until clear. Add crawfish tails. Cook, covered, over low heat about 15 to 20 minutes. Add crawfish fat and seasonings. Add parsley and onion tops and a small amount of hot water for desired consistency. Simmer for 20 minutes. Set aside before serving for about 20 minutes. Serve over rice. Enjoy!

Sue Abshire, a Soldiers' Angel in Baton Rouge, Louisiana

Crawfish Fettuccine

3 lb crawfish (or shrimp if crawfish not available) 1 pt half-and-half 3 onions 1 t fresh garlic 1 lb fettuccine noodles 1½ lb Velveeta ¼ c flour ¼ c grated Parmesan cheese green onions 1 can Rotel tomatoes 1½ sticks margarine 2 large bell peppers	Sauté the onions, bell peppers, and garlic in the butter. Stir in the crawfish, let cook on medium heat for about 10 minutes. Add half-and-half, tomatoes, and flour; stir well, and simmer for about 15 minutes. Melt in Velveeta. Cook fettuccine noodles according to the package, in separate pot. Stir in the green onions. Stir in cooked noodles. Put all in deep casserole dish; sprinkle with the Parmesan cheese. Bake for about 30 minutes at 350. Enjoy! This recipe can be made ahead up to the baking part and cooked at a later date. Also freezes well!

Cat Roule, a Soldiers' Angel in Denham Springs, Louisiana

Jambalaya

Ingredients	Instructions
1 T shortening 2 T flour 1 lb pure pork sausage, smoked or loose uncased sausage ½ c chopped bell pepper 3 c raw shrimp, peeled, deveined, and chopped 5 c tomatoes, diced and peeled 2½ c water 1 large onion, chopped 1 clove garlic, chopped 2 c raw rice 2 T Worcestershire sauce 1¼ t salt ½ t thyme ¼ t red pepper	Melt shortening in large heavy Dutch oven. Add flour and stir until blended; then add sausage (cut into bite-sized pieces) and bell pepper. Cook for 5 minutes. Add the shrimp, tomatoes, water, onions, garlic, and parsley. Bring to a boil; add rice; and stir in Worcestershire sauce, salt, thyme, and red pepper. Cover and simmer for 30 minutes, or until rice is tender. Stir occasionally.

Sue Abshire, a Soldiers' Angel in Baton Rouge, Louisiana

Maine

Banana Bread

¼ c shortening 1 t salt 1 c sugar 2 eggs 1½ c flour 1 t baking soda 3 bananas, beaten creamy	Cream shortening; add salt; add sugar gradually. Add eggs one at a time, beating well after each addition. Sift flour, measure, sift together with soda. Mash bananas with a fork, beat until light. Add alternately with sifted dry ingredients to egg mixture. No nuts in this recipe. Turn into greased loaf pan. Bake 1 hour at 350.

Shari Johnson, a Soldiers' Angel in Jacksonville, Florida

Blueberry Squares

3 c flour 2 c sugar, divided 1 t salt 3 T baking powder ½ c margarine 2 eggs 2 c Maine wild blueberries ½ c water 1½ T cornstarch	This recipe is from the Appalachian Trail Café. For crumb mixture, combine flour, 1 cup sugar, salt, and baking powder; cut in margarine. Add eggs and stir until crumbly. Put half of this mixture into bottom of 9x12 pan. Make filling from blueberries, water, cornstarch, and the other cup of sugar, cook until thickened. Spread filling over crumb mix. Cover with remainder of crumb mixture. Bake at 350 for 30 minutes.

Pheasantfarmer, a Soldiers' Angel in Maine

Fiddlehead Quiche Pie

1 single pie crust (use store bought) 1½ t Dijon mustard ¼ c chopped onion ¼ c sliced mushrooms ½ c half-and-half 1 T grated Parmesan cheese ⅛ t pepper 1½ c blanched fiddleheads 1 c shredded Swiss cheese 3 eggs ¾ c plain low-fat yogurt 2 t cornstarch ½ t salt ⅛ t nutmeg	Bake the pie crust at 350 for 10 minutes. Spread mustard on the bottom of the pie shell. Layer Swiss cheese in pie shell, then beat eggs, yogurt, half-and-half, onions, mushrooms, cheese, cornstarch, salt, pepper, nutmeg, and fiddleheads together and pour into shell. Put the rest of the Swiss cheese over the top. Bake at 350 for 40 to 45 minutes. Cool 10 minutes. This is a "wicked" good recipe! Enjoy the taste of Maine!

Sharon Mulligan, a Soldiers' Angel in Saco, Maine

Porcupine Meatballs

2 lb hamburger 2 cans tomatoes 1 c uncooked rice 2 c water 1 medium onion salt and pepper to taste	No animals were harmed in the making of this recipe! Mix all ingredients and form into meatballs. Cook in microwave 1 hour or until rice is done. Enjoy!

Mary Fowler, a Soldiers' Angel in Gardier, Maine

Raspberry Cottage Cheese Salad

1 medium container cottage cheese 1 large can crushed pineapple, drained well 1 large box raspberry Jell-O 1 small container frozen whipped topping, thawed	Drain pineapple well. Mix it with cottage cheese and Jell-O. Fold in whipped topping. Chill.

Mary Fowler, a Soldiers' Angel in Gardier, Maine

Maryland

Blue Crab Stuffed Mushrooms

1 lb Maryland backfin crab meat ⅓ c mayonnaise 1 egg 2 T milk 1 t Worcestershire sauce 1 t dry mustard ½ t celery salt ¼ t pepper ⅛ t paprika pinch ginger 2 T cracker meal 24 fresh mushrooms (about 2 - 3 inches in diameter) 1 c mayonnaise 1 egg ⅛ t Old Bay Seasoning 2 dashes liquid hot pepper paprika, for sprinkling	Remove cartilage from crabmeat, being careful not to break crab lumps. Place crabmeat in large bowl and set aside. In small bowl mix ½ cup mayonnaise, egg, milk, Worcestershire sauce, mustard, celery salt, pepper, paprika, and ginger. Pour sauce over crabmeat and mix gently, but thoroughly. Carefully mix in cracker meal. Wash and remove stems from mushrooms. Place mushrooms in a baking pan stem side up and fill each mushroom with about 2 tablespoons crab mixture. Place in a 375 oven for 10 to 12 minutes or until crabmeat mixtures begins to brown. Mix together 1 cup mayonnaise, egg, seafood seasoning, and liquid hot pepper sauce. Spread a generous amount of topping over each mushroom. Sprinkle with paprika and bake at 375 oven until the topping becomes a light brown color, approximately 5 to 7 minutes.

Jennifer German, a Soldiers' Angel in Bowie, Maryland

Catfish Chowder

1 lb catfish fillets, cut into chunks 2 slices bacon, chopped 1 c chopped onion 1 can sliced potatoes, drained 1 can diced tomatoes 2 c water 1 can corn, drained ¼ t tarragon ½ t celery salt 2 t parsley flakes ½ t oregano ¼ t salt pepper to taste 1 t Old Bay Seasoning 2 t thyme	In a large pot, cook bacon until crisp. Add onions and cook until soft. Add potatoes, tomatoes, and 2 cups water. Cover and simmer until potatoes are tender. Add corn and seasonings. Slowly simmer and adjust seasonings to taste. Add catfish 5 to 10 minutes before serving and simmer.

Jennifer German, a Soldiers' Angel in Bowie, Maryland

Cheese Steak Egg Rolls

1 lb sirloin steak, sliced thin (or steakums) 1½ c mushrooms/onions/peppers (optional) ¼ c plus 3 T steak marinade 1 c mayonnaise ¼ c sour cream 1 (16-oz) pkg egg roll wrappers American cheese slices	Brown steak, drain, and return to pan. Add veggies and cook until tender. Stir in ¼ cup steak marinade, stirring frequently until thickened. Meanwhile, combine mayonnaise, sour cream, and 3 tablespoons steak marinade. Set aside. Arrange egg roll wrappers with corner facing you with 1 or ½ slice of American cheese, and about 2 tablespoons of steak mixture. Brush edges of wrapper with water. Roll tightly and set aside. On cookie sheet, arrange egg roll wrappers seam side down. Spray each egg roll with nonstick cooking spray. Bake at 425, turning once, for 16 minutes or until golden.

Dina Boebel, a Soldiers' Angel in Bel Air, Maryland

Corn Chowder

1 can chicken broth 1 c diced potato 1 c diced carrots 1 can skim evaporated milk (or regular) 1 can cream corn few T potato flakes	Cook potato and carrots in broth until tender. Add milk, corn, and potato flakes to thicken the soup. This is easy and great tasting!

Mary Owens, a Soldiers' Angel in Maryland

Crab Cakes

1 lb Maryland backfin crabmeat
1 c Italian-seasoned bread crumbs
1 large egg, beaten
¼ c mayonnaise
1 t Worcestershire sauce
1 t good old yellow mustard
½ t salt
¼ t pepper
½ t seafood seasoning (optional)
butter or oil for frying

In mixing bowl, blend all ingredients except crabmeat. Add crabmeat, fold in gently, but mix thoroughly. Shape into cakes. Cook in fry pan until browned; about 5 minutes on each side. Or wrap crab cakes and place in freezer until you cook them.

Leanne, a Soldiers' Angel in Maryland

Crabs and Linguine

6 crabs, steamed
1 lb crab meat (optional)
2 whole garlic cloves, halved
¼ c olive oil
¼ t basil
½ t Old Bay Seasoning
2 lb cans crushed tomatoes
1 (6-oz) can tomato paste
1 lb linguine
grated cheese, for serving

Pull off backs of crabs and remove all gills. Thoroughly clean crabs. Break them in half, but do not remove meat. In large pot, brown garlic until soft. Add all the ingredients (except linguine), adding water if too thick. Simmer at least 1 hour, or longer. Cook linguine al dente. Drain, place in large bowl. Add half the sauce. Reserve remainder of sauce for individual servings. Top with grated cheese if desired. Note: Sauce tastes better as it cooks. I prefer to cook mine for 6 or more hours, refrigerate, and serve the next day.

Dina, a Soldiers' Angel in Bel Air, Maryland

Honey Bun Cake

Ingredients	Instructions
1 (18.25 oz) box plain yellow cake mix 1 c sour cream ¾ c vegetable oil 4 large eggs ⅓ c honey ⅓ c packed light brown sugar 1 T ground cinnamon ½ c finely chopped pecans (optional) 2 c confectioners' sugar, sifted ⅓ c milk 1 t pure vanilla extract	Place a rack in center of oven and preheat to 350. Lightly spray a 13 x 9 baking pan. Place cake mix, sour cream, oil, and eggs in a large mixing bowl. Blend with electric mixer on low for 1 minute. Scrap sides often. Continue mixing on medium for another 2 minutes. Batter should look thick and well blended. Pour into prepared pan. Drizzle honey on top of batter, then sprinkle on the brown sugar, cinnamon, and pecans. If you desire, you can swirl knife through this mixture. Bake until golden brown (38 to 40 minutes). Place on wire rack. For the glaze, place the confectioners' sugar, milk, and vanilla in a small mixing bowl and stir until the mixture is well combined. Pour the glaze over the top of the hot cake in the pan; spread to sides with a spoon. Cool cake 20 minutes longer before serving. You can store the cake covered in plastic wrap at room temperature for up to 1 week. You can freeze it wrapped in aluminum foil for up to 6 months. Thaw overnight before serving frozen cake. Enjoy!

Pat Palmer, a Soldiers' Angel in Fallston, Maryland

Southern Maryland Stuffed Ham

1 (20 - 22-lb) corned ham, boned 10 lb cabbage 1 - 1½ lb kale 3 lb onion 2½ - 3 T crushed red pepper 1 - 1½ T black pepper 1 pkg cheesecloth	Trim excess fat from ham. Preheat oven to 400. Wash cabbage, kale, and onions with cold water. Chop or shred cabbage, kale, and onions and place in a large bowl. Add red and black pepper. Mix all ingredients thoroughly. Prepare ham for stuffing by making 1- or 2-inch slits all over the ham, about 1 to 2 inches deep. Using a gloved hand, press stuffing into slits until full. Fill large cavity where bone was located with stuffing also. When finished stuffing, tie ham with string. Wrap ham with cheesecloth and tie securely. Cover ham with aluminum foil and bake for 5 hours. When ham is finished, drain and let ham cool down overnight in the refrigerator before carving. Serve cold.

Jennifer German, a Soldiers' Angel in Bowie, Maryland

Massachusetts

Boston Baked Beans

1 lb navy or pea beans 1 large onion, chopped 2 T Dijon mustard ¼ c dark brown sugar ⅓ c light brown sugar ¼ c molasses 1 t salt, or to taste	Discard any discolored beans. In a large bowl, combine the beans with plenty of cold water and soak overnight for 6 to 8 hours. Drain the beans. In a large pot, combine the beans and enough water to cover them by 1 inch. Bring to a boil, lower the heat to simmer, and cook for 45 minutes or until they are just tender (it may take longer if the beans are old or the soaking time was short). Drain the beans and set aside the cooking liquid. Set the oven at 325. In a bean pot or deep casserole with a lid, combine the beans, onion, mustard, dark and light brown sugars, molasses, and salt. Add enough of the cooking liquid to just cover the beans. Stir to blend them. Bring the liquid to a boil on top of the stove, then transfer to the oven and bake for 2 hours, checking every 30 minutes to make sure the beans don't dry. Add more cooking liquid if necessary. When the beans are tender, uncover the pot and cook for 20 to 30 minutes more to make a slightly crusty top.

Mother, a Soldiers' Angel in Salem, New Hampshire

Cranberry Muffins

2 c flour 2 t baking powder ½ t salt 1 stick butter, softened 1 c sugar 2 eggs, warmed to room temperature 1 c orange juice 1½ c fresh cranberries, chopped ¾ c chopped walnuts	Preheat oven to 375. Line muffin tins with papers. Makes about 18 to 24 muffins. In small bowl, mix together flour, baking powder, and salt. Set aside. Set eggs in bowl of warm water for 10 minutes. Meanwhile, in large mixing bowl, beat sugar and butter until fluffy. Add eggs, one at a time, beating well after each egg. Add half of orange juice and beat well. Add half of flour and beat well. Repeat, using up the remaining juice and flour alternately. Fold in cranberries and nuts. Fill muffin cups 2/3 full. Bake 25 minutes or until done. (Muffins will not rise high but will stay somewhat flat. Be careful not to burn the bottoms)

L Hunt, a Soldiers' Angel in Medfield, Massachusetts

Fish Chowder

1 medium onion, chopped 5 - 6 medium potatoes, cubed 3 chicken bouillon cubes (or equivalent in powder) salt and pepper 2 cans evaporated milk 1½ lb fish (I use haddock) ⅓ - ½ butter, sliced	Place potatoes and onions in large pot, cover with just enough water to cook them and add bouillon cubes and a little salt and pepper. When potatoes are cooked, lay fish on top, cover and leave on medium heat until fish is flaky. When fish is cooked, cut up with a spoon into chunks. Add 2 cans evaporated milk and butter and stir together until butter is melted.

Sherry Wiemann, a Soldiers' Angel in Tauton, Massachusetts

Irish Soda Bread

4 c flour 2 T sugar 1 T baking powder 1 t baking soda 1 t salt ½ c (liquid) vegetable oil 1 c raisins 1 c buttermilk 1 egg extra oil for top of loaf	Preheat oven to 350. In large bowl, sift dry ingredients. Add oil to flour mixture and mix with fork or pastry blender until fine crumbs form (about pea-sized lumps). Stir in raisins. In separate bowl, mix milk and egg together, beating lightly. Gradually add to flour mixture, stirring until soft dough forms. Turn dough onto floured board and knead lightly about 10 times, or until smooth. Shape into ball and place onto greased cookie sheet. Flatten ball slightly and cut a large "X" into the top. Brush top of loaf with oil. Bake for 50 to 60 minutes, or until top is brown. Cool on wire rack.

L Hunt, a Soldiers' Angel in Medfield, Massachusetts

Leftovers from Clambake

1 can chopped clams with juice (or use clams leftover from clambake) 2 - 4 hot dogs/sliced into thin coins 4 - 6 breakfast sausages, cut up ½ lb chorizo sausage or kielbasa, sliced into coins 4 medium potatoes, red or white, diced 1 onion, sliced thin 1 t crushed hot pepper salt and pepper to taste	Put everything in soup pan/stock pot. Add more water, enough to cover all ingredients. Over low heat and covered, cook for about 1 hour, until potatoes and onions are done. Also works well in a crock pot. Serve with saltines/oyster crackers/crusty bread, or the like.

Kim, a Soldiers' Angel in Massachusetts

Pumpkin Bread

3½ c flour 2 t salt 2 t baking soda 1 t baking powder 1 t cinnamon 1 t ground nutmeg 3 c sugar 1 c (liquid) vegetable oil 4 eggs 1 can pumpkin (about 2 c) 1 c chopped walnuts butter or cream cheese, for serving	Preheat oven to 350. In large bowl, combine dry ingredients and blend together. Add in remaining ingredients and beat well to combine. Grease and flour 3 to 4 1-lb coffee cans* (carefully!). Pour batter into each can, filling about 2/3 full. Place cans on lower oven rack and bake 1 to 1½ hours, until top has risen up and become dark brown, forming a crispy crust. Remove from oven and cool completely before removing from coffee cans. Slice into ½ -inch circles to serve. Can be eaten plain, with butter or with cream cheese. *Can use loaf pans or bundt pan

L Hunt, a Soldiers' Angel in Medfield, Massachusetts

Slow Cooker Taco Soup

1 pkg Hidden Valley ranch dressing mix
1 pkg taco seasoning mix (I use the
    reduced sodium one)
1 medium onion, chopped
1 lb ground beef (or turkey)
1 can corn
1 can black beans
1 can pinto beans
1 can Italian stewed tomatoes
1 can Rotel tomatoes
1 can beef broth (I use the low sodium/low
    fat one)
sour cream, shredded jack cheese, and
    nachos, for serving

Brown together the ground beef and chopped onion. Drain and add to slow cooker. Add Rotel and Italian tomatoes. (You can crush these with your hand to make the bits smaller if you're family doesn't like big chunks.) Add the ranch dressing mix and taco mix and stir well. Drain the liquid from the corn, black beans, and pinto beans and rinse with cold water. (This helps reduce the sodium.) Add the can of beef broth and stir well. Cook in the slow cooker for 8 to 9 hours on low or 5 hours on high. You can serve this with a scoop of sour cream and shredded jack cheese and crumble nachos on top.
Note: You can also cook on stove top for about an hour or so, but the flavor really tastes better in a slow cooker.

Sherry Wiemann, a Soldiers' Angel in Tauton, Massachusetts

Michigan

Authentic Pasty Recipe

2 c flour ⅔ c shortening ½ t salt ½ c cold water ¾ lb ground chuck or ½-inch cubes of steak ½ c chopped onion ½ c grated rutabaga (or carrots) ½ c grated (edible) beef suet (optional) (the suet is used with the lean steak, and can be traded off to the fat content of the ground beef) 3 c diced potatoes 1½ t salt ½ t pepper 2 T dried parsley or ⅓ c chopped fresh milk, for brushing pastry	The proper pronunciation is PAWSTEA. In a large bowl, cut shortening into flour, add ½ teaspoon salt and water. Mix and knead until well blended. Form into 4 balls and chill in the refrigerator for at least 1 hour. On counter-top roll each ball into 8-inch circle. Use plenty of flour while rolling out. Mix the filling together in a large bowl (beef, onion, rutabaga, suet, potatoes, salt, pepper, and parsley). On the rolled out dough, brush the edges with milk. Put 1 cup of filling onto 1 side of each crust and fold the remaining side over. Seal the edge by pressing with a fork. Put on cookie sheet, cut 1 slit (1/2 inch) in each for steam to escape and brush top with milk. Bake in 400 oven on bottom shelf for 25 minutes, then move to middle shelf for 20 minutes.

SueAnn Hardiman, a Soldiers' Angel in Gwinn, Michigan

Balsamic Pork and Berry Salad

6 c torn romaine 2 c sliced fresh strawberries ½ c thinly sliced celery 1 t snipped fresh chives 8 oz pork tenderloin (or chicken/turkey breasts) 1 t olive oil or salad oil 2 cloves garlic, minced ¼ c honey ¼ c balsamic vinegar ¼ t pepper 2 T chopped pecans or walnuts, toasted	This recipe calls for pork tenderloin, but we've substituted chicken or turkey breast slices many times. We've also substituted berries other than strawberries. Raspberries and blueberries are a good combo too! In a large mixing bowl, toss romaine, strawberries, celery, and chives. Set aside. Trim any fat from pork. Grill pork until completely cooked. If cooking indoors and not on the grill, cut pork into medallions, Coat an unheated large skillet with nonstick cooking spray. Preheat over medium-high heat. Add half of the pork; cook for 3 to 4 minutes or until pork is thoroughly cooked, turning once. Repeat with remaining pork. Remove all pork from skillet. Cover to keep warm. For dressing, add oil to skillet. Add garlic; cook and stir for 15 seconds. Stir in honey, vinegar, and pepper. Cook and stir until heated through. Place romaine mixture on 4 plates. Top with the pork. Drizzle dressing over. Sprinkle with pecans or walnuts. Serve immediately.

Min Kwiatkowski, a Soldiers' Angel in Lake Orion, Michigan

Cherry Dump Cake

1 (20-oz) can crushed pineapple 1 can cherry pie filling 1 box yellow or white cake mix 1 stick butter ½ c chopped nuts (optional) whipped cream or ice cream, for serving	Dump crushed pineapple in 9 x 13 inch pan (juice and all). Dump a can of cherry pie filling on top of pineapple. Spread cake mix (dry) over the above ingredients but do not mix. Dot pieces of butter over the cake mix; nuts may be added not or after baking. Bake at 350 for 30 to 45 minutes or until brown and the cake mix is absorbed in the fruit. Let cool and serve with either whipped cream or ice cream. Other fruit combinations could be used.

Sharon, a Soldiers' Angel in Michigan

Chicken Casserole

4 c cubed chicken 2 c celery 1½ c mayonnaise 1 can cream of chicken soup 1 c diced onion ⅔ c sliced almonds ½ stick butter 2 c shredded cheese rice, for serving	Sauté celery and onion in butter. Mix all ingredients, except cheese, and bake at 350 for 30 minutes. Remove from oven and top with cheese and bake for 15 minutes. Serve on a bed of rice.

Sheri Lee-Cornett, a Soldiers' Angel in Dewitt, Michigan

Chicken Milano

1 T butter
2 cloves garlic, minced
½ c sun-dried tomatoes, chopped
1 c chicken broth, divided
1 c heavy cream
1 lb skinless, boneless chicken breast
    halves
salt and pepper to taste
2 T vegetable oil
2 T chopped fresh basil
8 oz dry fettuccini pasta

In a large saucepan over low heat, melt butter; add garlic and cook for 30 seconds. Add the tomatoes and 3/4 cup of chicken broth; increase to medium heat and bring to a boil. Reduce heat and simmer, uncovered, for about 10 minutes or until the tomatoes are tender. Add the cream and bring to a boil; stirring. Simmer over medium heat until the sauce is thick enough to coat the back of a spoon. Sprinkle the chicken with salt and pepper on both sides. In a large skillet over medium heat, warm oil and sauté chicken. Press on chicken occasionally with a slotted spatula. Cook for about 4 minutes per side or until the meat feels springy and is no longer pink inside. Transfer to a board; cover and keep warm. Discard the fat from the skillet. In the same skillet, over medium heat, bring 1/4 cup chicken broth to a boil; stirring the pan juices. Reduce slightly and add to the cream sauce; stir in basil and adjust seasonings to taste. Meanwhile, bring a large pot of lightly salted water to a boil. Add fettuccine and cook for 8 to 10 minutes or until al dente; drain, transfer to a bowl and toss with 3 to 4 tablespoons of the sauce. Cut each chicken breast into 2 to 3 diagonal slices. Reheat the sauce gently if needed. Transfer the pasta to serving plates; top with chicken and coat with the cream sauce; serve.

Min Kwiatkowski, a Soldiers' Angel in Lake Orion, Michigan

Cow Chip Pie

2 eggs
½ c flour
½ c white sugar
½ c brown sugar
1 c melted butter
1 (6-oz) pkg chocolate chips
1 unbaked pie shell
whipped cream or ice cream, for serving

Preheat oven to 325. In a large bowl, beat eggs until foamy. Beat in flour and sugars until well blended. Blend in melted butter; stir in chocolate chips and pour into pie shell. Bake for approximately 1 hour. Serve with whipped cream or ice cream.

Vicky Brolick, a Soldiers' Angel in Blanchard, Michigan

Goody Good Cookies

1 c oil
1 c oleo
1 c white sugar
1 c brown sugar
1 egg
1 T sour milk (few drops vinegar in regular
    milk)
1 t baking soda
3½ c flour or more
1 t salt
1 c oatmeal
1 c cornflakes
1½ c chocolate chips
½ c nuts

Combine oil, oleo, sugars, egg, milk, baking soda, flour, and salt. Add oatmeal, cornflakes, chocolate chips, and nuts. Drop on cookie sheet by teaspoon and press down and bake at 350 for 12 to 15 minutes.

Vicky Brolick, a Soldiers' Angel in Blanchard, Michigan

Hungarian Chicken Paprikash

4 chicken breasts with bone and skin (you can use boneless/skinless also) 1 c half-and-half (or ½ pt sour cream) 1 onion, chopped 2 T shortening/olive oil 1 T paprika 1 t black pepper 2 t salt 1 - 1½ c water 3 eggs, beaten 3 c flour ½ c water	Brown onion in shortening. Add seasonings and chicken; brown 10 minutes. Add water, cover, and let simmer slowly until tender. Remove chicken; add half-and-half to drippings and mix well. Heat and serve. For more gravy add more half-and-half or sour cream. For dumplings, mix ½ cup water, eggs, and flour and beat with spoon. Drop bits of batter in boiling salted water. Cook about 10 minutes; drain and rinse with cold water. Drain well and add to paprikash.

Min Kwiatkowski, a Soldiers' Angel in Lake Orion, Michigan

Mom's Date-filled Cookies

1 c butter ½ c sugar ½ c brown sugar 2 eggs 3 t milk ½ t soda 3 c flour 1 t vanilla Filling: 1½ c chopped dates ½ c sugar ½ c water ½ c walnuts	Cream butter, sugar, brown sugar, eggs, and milk. Add soda, flour, and vanilla. Roll out and cut into circles. For filling, combine dates, sugar, water, and walnuts. Cook 4 to 5 minutes. Put 1 teaspoon on each circle and fold over to make a half circle. Bake at 350 for 15 minutes.

Sheri Lee-Cornett, a Soldiers' Angel in Dewitt, Michigan

Northern Potato Soup

10 medium-to-large potatoes 1 large white onion, chopped 1 lb bacon (or ham) ½ t black pepper milk	Peel, wash, and dice the potatoes. Place in water and set on medium. Take bacon and cut it into medium-size pieces; cook the bacon until crisp, save the drippings. When potatoes are just barely tender, put bacon in the water and add some of the drippings. Add onion; turn heat down to medium low and let slowly simmer for about an hour. Add pepper and about 2 cups of milk. It is good for those cold frigid days. Serve with grilled cheese. An added twist: you can add about a cup of cubed processed cheese to it for the last half hour with the milk to make a cheesy tater soup!

jayde1031, a Soldiers' Angel in Mississippi

Santa Fe Chicken Tortellini Casserole

9 oz cheese tortellini 1 T olive oil 2 c broccoli flowerets ½ c onion, chopped 1 c red bell pepper 3 T flour 2 T olive oil ¾ c chicken broth ¾ c milk 1 t ground cumin ¼ t cayenne pepper 4 c cooked chicken, cut up ¾ c Monterey Jack cheese, shredded ½ c Colby cheese, shredded ½ c tortilla chips, crushed	Heat oven to 325. Cook and drain tortellini as directed on the package. While tortellini is cooking, grease 3-quart casserole dish. Heat 1 tablespoon of oil in skillet over medium heat. Cook broccoli, onion, and bell pepper in oil for 3 minutes, stirring frequently, until crisp-tender. Remove broccoli mixture from skillet. Cook flour and 2 tablespoons oil in same skillet over low heat, stirring constantly, until smooth. Stir in milk, broth, and cumin. Heat to boiling over medium heat, stirring constantly; remove from heat. Stir in chicken, Monterey Jack cheese, and the tortellini and broccoli mixture. Spoon tortellini mixture into casserole dish. Bake uncovered 25 to 35 minutes or until bubbly. During the last 5 minutes of baking, sprinkle cayenne pepper, Colby cheese, and tortilla chips over the top. Bake until cheese is melted. Leftovers are AWESOME and this freezes GREAT!!!

Min Kwiatkowski, a Soldiers' Angel in Lake Orion, Michigan

Minnesota

Chicken Wild Rice Salad

⅔ c mayonnaise
⅓ c milk
2 T lemon juice
¼ t dried tarragon, crumbled
3 c cooked, cubed chicken
3 c cooked wild rice
⅓ c finely sliced green onion
1 (8-oz) can sliced water chestnuts, drained
½ t salt
⅛ t pepper
1 c seedless green grape halves
1 c salted cashews
grape clusters, for serving

In small bowl, blend mayonnaise, milk, lemon juice, and tarragon; set aside. In large bowl, combine chicken, wild rice, green onion, water chestnuts, salt, and pepper. Stir in mayonnaise mixture until blended. Refrigerate, covered, 2 to 3 hours. Just before serving, fold in grapes and cashews. Garnish with clusters of grapes. One cup uncooked wild rice equals 3 to 4 cups cooked. There is cooked wild rice in a can that works well, the brand is Canoe. To speed things up, if you want to use mixed white and dark meat you can use a rotisserie chicken. If you want to use just chicken breast, KFC works just fine.

Dillysgrammy, a Soldiers' Angel in Minnesota

Chippy Bars

½ c oil
1½ c graham cracker crumbs
1⅔ c peanut butter chips
1½ c flaked coconut
1 can sweetened condensed milk
1 c chocolate chips
1½ t shortening

Preheat oven to 350. Place oil in a 13 x 9 inch pan put in oven to melt. Remove and add graham crumbs evenly in pan; press down. Layer 1 cup peanut butter chips over crumbs; sprinkle coconut over chips and drizzle milk evenly over top. Bake 20 minutes. In microwave, melt chocolate chips and shortening. Drizzle over bars. Cut into about 4 dozen bars because they are a little rich.

Janet Seabern, a Soldiers' Angel in Winona, Minnesota

Lefse

4 heaping c mashed or riced potatoes 1 stick butter ⅓ c milk 1 t sugar 1 t salt 2 c flour extra flour, for rolling out the dough butter, for serving sugar or cinnamon sugar, for serving	It isn't Christmas without lefse. Measure the potatoes into a bowl. In saucepan, melt the butter in the milk; stir in the sugar and salt. Pour over the cold potatoes and mix. Stir 2 cups of flour into the potato mixture. The dough will be sticky and soft. Start heating the griddle or electric frying pan. Do not add any oil, margarine, or shortening. Lefse is baked on a dry surface. Take a lump of dough about the size of an egg. Place a heaping teaspoon of flour on the work surface. Work about half of the heaping teaspoon of flour into the lump of dough (enough so you can handle the dough, but not so much that the dough becomes dry). Starting in the center, roll outward until the lefse is about the size of a dinner plate. Try not to roll the lefse so thin that you cannot pick it up. If the lefse tears when you start to pick it up, gather it into a lump and roll it out again. Ideally, you should only roll the lefse once. Turn the lefse only once while rolling. If the lefse starts to stick, add a little more flour. When the lefse is rolled out, transfer it to the hot griddle. Bake it for about 1 minute, just until brown freckles start to appear; then turn the lefse over and let the other side bake just until brown freckles start to appear. While the first piece of lefse is baking, roll out your second one. After the first piece of lefse is done, use the pancake turner to remove it from the griddle and place it on a clean dishtowel. Cover with another dishtowel. Repeat until you have baked all of the dough. Place each newly baked lefse on top of the previously baked lefse and cover the stack with the towel. Once the lefse is completely cool, place it in a plastic bag or wrap it with plastic wrap or aluminum foil to help keep it moist. When you're ready to eat lefse, spread it with butter, sprinkle sugar on it (some people also like to sprinkle cinnamon on their lefse), and roll into a log. Can be frozen and reheated with butter and sugar in microwave.

Alice, a Soldiers' Angel in St Cloud, Minnesota

Norwegian Meatballs

5 lb ground meat (beef, veal, pork; ground 3 times) 2 medium onions, finely ground (save juice) ½ t nutmeg ½ t allspice 1 T salt ½ t pepper 2 eggs, beaten ½ c half-and-half ½ c cracker meal or matzo meal 4 - 5 beef bouillon cubes or 4 - 5 t instant beef bouillon 2 t Kitchen Bouquet flour	Heat oven to 350. Combine all meatball ingredients; knead by hand 5 minutes or more to blend spices into meat. Lightly grease or coat shallow baking pans with no-stick cooking spray. Form small round meat balls; dipping hands into cold water to shape smooth. Bake 10 to 15 minutes. Place meatballs in large kettle; add bouillon cubes, meat drippings from baking pan and water to cover. Stir in Kitchen Bouquet. Heat to boiling; reduce heat and simmer 1 hour. Remove meatballs. Thicken gravy with flour to desired consistency.

Anne Hartley, a Soldiers' Angel in Texas

Tater Tot Hotdish

2 lb hamburger 1 can cream of mushroom soup 1 can of any veggie 1 c milk 2 c shredded Cheddar cheese bag of tater tots	Mix all ingredients together except for 1 cup shredded Cheddar cheese and the tater tots. Put tater tots on top of mixture, sprinkle remaining cup of cheese over tater tots. Put in the oven at 350 and bake until tater tots are golden brown. This is my favorite 'DUMP' meal ever because you 'DUMP' it all together!

Angel, a Soldiers' Angel in Shakopee, Minnesota

Teriyaki Chicken

2 lb boneless chicken skinless chicken breasts 1 pkg frozen broccoli, carrots, water chestnuts 2 T quick-cooking tapioca 1 c chicken broth 4 T brown sugar 4 T teriyaki sauce 2 T dry mustard 1½ t grated orange peel 1 t ground ginger hot cooked rice, for serving	Rinse chicken and dry; cut chicken into 1-inch pieces. Place frozen vegetables in crock pot and sprinkle with tapioca. Place chicken pieces on top of vegetables. In small bowl, mix chicken broth, brown sugar, teriyaki sauce, mustard, orange peel, and ginger. Pour sauce over chicken. Cover, cook on low 4 to 6 hour or on high 2 to 3 hours. Serve over hot cooked rice.

Janet Seabern, a Soldiers' Angel in Winona, Minnesota

Mississippi

Cornbread Salad

1 (8½-oz) pkg cornbread muffin mix
1 (1-oz) envelope Ranch-style salad
    dressing mix
1 (8-oz) container sour cream
1 c mayonnaise
3 large tomatoes, chopped
½ c chopped red bell pepper
½ c chopped green bell pepper
½ c chopped green onions
2 (16-oz) cans pinto beans, drained
2 c shredded Cheddar cheese
10 slices bacon, cooked and crumbled
2 (15 ¼-oz) cans whole kernel corn,
    drained

Prepare cornbread muffin mix according to package directions; cool. Stir together salad dressing mix, sour cream, and mayonnaise until blended; set aside. Combine tomatoes, peppers, and green onions and gently toss. Crumble half the cornbread into a 3-quart trifle bowl or large salad bowl. Top with half each of beans, tomato mixture, cheese, bacon, corn, and dressing mixture; repeat layers. Cover and chill 3 hours.

Rhonda McKenzie, a Soldiers' Angel in Kokomo, Mississippi

Cucumber Sandwich Spread (Finger Sandwiches)

1 (8-oz) package cream cheese
1 large cucumber, peeled, grated, and
    drained
1 T grated onion
2 T mayonnaise
few drops of lemon juice
½ t dill weed
dash of salt and pepper
drop of green food coloring

Mix well and spread on thin sliced bread using 3 slices for each sandwich. Wrap closely in foil, seal in plastic bag, and freeze until party time. Thaw, then remove crust, slice thin into finger sandwiches. Each large sandwich will make 4 finger sandwiches. If you wish to use this spread as a dip for crackers, add the juice from the cucumber and more mayonnaise.

Cheryl Bailey, a Soldiers' Angel in Amory, Mississippi

Mississippi Chili

2 large onions, coarsely chopped, more to taste 4 ribs celery, coarsely chopped 2 cloves garlic, minced oil 1½ lb coarsely ground beef 2 T chili powder, more to taste ½ t ground cumin, more to taste 1 (24-oz) can tomato juice 2 (15-oz) cans kidney beans salt and pepper to taste	Sauté onions, celery, and garlic in small amount of oil. Transfer to deep pot. Brown meat and add to pot. Add seasoning and tomato juice and mix. Drain kidney beans and reserve liquid. Add bean liquid to pot, and salt and pepper to taste. Simmer 2 hours. Add kidney beans and simmer until thick.

Rhonda McKenzie, a Soldiers' Angel in Kokomo, Mississippi

Mississippi Mud Bars

2 c unsalted butter, room temperature, divided 2 c sugar 4 eggs, room temperature 2 t vanilla 1½ c all-purpose flour ¼ c + ⅓ c cocoa ½ t salt ¾ c flaked coconut 1 (7-oz) jar marshmallow crème 4 c powdered sugar ½ c evaporated milk	Heat oven to 350. Lightly grease a 9 x 13-inch baking pan. Beat 1 ½ cups butter and sugar until fluffy. Beat in eggs, one at a time, and 1 teaspoon vanilla. Sift flour, ¼ cup cocoa, and salt. Stir this mixture into egg mixture, and then stir in coconut. Spread evenly in pan. Bake 35 to 40 minutes or until a toothpick inserted in the middle comes out clean. Remove and spoon crème over the top. Spread evenly and set aside. Cool completely before icing. For icing, beat ½ cup butter and 1 teaspoon vanilla. Combine powdered sugar and 1/3 cup cocoa and gradually beat into butter mixture, alternating with milk. Spread over cooled brownies. When the icing sets, cut the brownies into pieces.

Rhonda McKenzie, a Soldiers' Angel in Kokomo, Mississippi

Mississippi Pecan Pie

1 c white corn syrup (dark if you like it rich) 1 c pecans ½ c sugar 3 eggs 1 t vanilla ½ t salt 9-inch unbaked pastry shell vanilla ice cream, for serving hot fudge sauce, for serving	Preheat oven to 325 while mixing ingredients. Place syrup, pecans, sugar, slightly beaten eggs, vanilla, and salt in bowl and stir to combine ingredients. Pour into the unbaked 9-inch pastry shell and bake 50 minutes at 325 degrees. Pecans will float to the top forming a crust that will brown as it slowly bakes. Serve with vanilla ice cream and or a drizzle of hot fudge for a special treat.

Cheryl Bailey, a Soldiers' Angel in Amory, Mississippi

Slow Cooker Mac n Cheese

2 lb elbow macaroni 2 c milk 3 - 4 bags shredded cheese, any type or mixture 2 eggs	Now remember I have 4 sons, 3 of which are teenagers so my ingredients are for serving HUGE appetites! Cook the elbow macaroni about half way; it should still be pretty firm. Place it in a crock pot. Mix the eggs and milk and add to the macaroni. Add 3/4 of cheese leaving a little to put on the top before serving. Stir well and let cook for about 2 to 3 hours. Thirty minutes before serving, put the remaining cheese on top. I've added ham to this, bacon, hamburger, chicken and tuna to make a complete meal.

jayde1031, a Soldiers' Angel in Mississippi

Missouri

Girdle Buster

1 c flour 1 stick butter 1½ c pecans, divided 2 small containers frozen whipped topping 1½ c powdered sugar 1 pkg cream cheese 1 pkg instant chocolate pudding 1 pkg instant vanilla pudding 3 c milk	Cut the butter into the flour (will have pea-sized lumps); add 1 cup pecans. Press into baking dish and bake at 350 for 20 minutes. Let cool. Mix powdered sugar and cream cheese, fold in 1 container of thawed whipped topping, and place on first layer. (I have noticed it mixes better if you let the cream cheese get to room temperature.) For the third layer, mix milk and both instant pudding mixes (beat with mixer until thickens) place on top of second layer. For the top layer, spread the other container of thawed whipped topping and sprinkle ½ cup pecans over the top. Feel free to use any kind of instant pudding mix. Strawberry, lemon or any other. I would be careful mixing the puddings if using a different flavor. Strawberry and chocolate. Vanilla will go with about anything. Enjoy.

Melanie Henry, a Soldiers' Angel in New Madrid, Missouri

Happy Apple Cake

1 box yellow cake mix 1¼ c water ¼ c oil ⅓ c butter, softened 4 eggs ½ c graham cracker crumbs 2 t cinnamon ¼ c quick oats 3 medium apples, peeled and chopped ¼ c butter ¼ c brown sugar Topping: 1 c graham cracker crumbs ⅓ c melted butter ¼ c brown sugar	It's like having a caramel apple inside your cake!! Simply delicious. Heat oven to 350. Grease and flour 13 x 9 x 2 inch rectangular pan. Mix cake mix (dry), water, oil, butter, eggs, oats, and graham cracker crumbs in large bowl on low speed. Scrape bowl frequently. Fold in cooked apples. Prepare apples by cooking them until tender over medium heat with 1/4 cup brown sugar and 1/4 cup butter. Pour mix into pan; sprinkle evenly with topping. Bake until cake pulls away from sides of pan and wooden pick inserted in center comes out clean, 38 to 43 minutes; cool completely. Topping: Blend with a pastry cutter 1 cup graham cracker crumbs, 1/3 cup softened butter, and 1/4 cup brown sugar.

Srpalmer63, a Soldiers' Angel in Missouri

Missouri Fudge Cake

4 rounded T cocoa 1 c margarine, softened 1 c water 2 c flour 2 c sugar ½ t salt 2 eggs 1 t baking soda 1 t vanilla ½ c buttermilk Frosting: ½ c margarine 4 rounded T cocoa 1 lb powdered sugar 6 T milk 1 t vanilla 1 c Missouri pecans	Boil cocoa, margarine, and water. Add flour, sugar, and salt. Mix eggs, baking soda, vanilla, and buttermilk and add. Pour onto a large rimmed cookie sheet (11 x 17 x 1). Bake at 350 for 20 minutes. Mix margarine, cocoa, powdered sugar, milk, vanilla, and pecans and pour on cake while it is still warm.

Srpalmer63, a Soldiers' Angel in Missouri

Montana

Montana Special

3 lb venison roast 1 good-sized onion 1 can tomatoes, no. 303 1 c water 1 can tomato hot sauce salt and pepper to taste flour garlic salt oil or shortening	Trim the roast of fat and bad spots. Cut the roast as thin as possible. Sprinkle salt, pepper, and garlic both sides of each piece of the roast. Then flour both sides. Use enough oil or shortening to cover the bottom of fry pan. Heat, brown on both sides. Put the pieces in a roaster or covered pan. Put the rest of the ingredients over the top the roast and bake in the oven at 300 for about 3 hours or until done. Take the meat out and use the rest for gravy.

Donna Allon (fefifauxfumgirl), a Soldiers' Angel in Alabama

Nebraska

Grandma Pat's Sugar Cookies

3 c flour 2 t baking powder 1 t soda ½ t nutmeg 1 c margarine 2 eggs 1 c sugar 4 T milk 1 t vanilla ½ t burnt sugar flavoring vanilla cream icing, for frosting cookies	Cream margarine and sugar, add eggs, milk, vanilla, and burnt sugar flavoring. Mix the dry ingredients in a separate bowl. Add the dry ingredients to the sugar/butter mixture. Refrigerate for at least 2 hours. Roll out to about ¼-inch thickness. Cut with desired cookie cutter. Bake 350 for about 8 minutes (until just golden brown around the edges). Cool. Frost with vanilla cream icing (adding any food coloring desired).

Pat Gericke, Nebraska

Nebraska Volcano Punch

½ gal apricot nectar 1 gal pineapple juice 4 L Sprite 1 qt grain alcohol 6 sliced apples (to float in punch)	Mix the ingredients together in a large punch bowl or container. Place the sliced apples to float in the punch. Note: Be careful eating the apples! For some reason, the grain alcohol seems to get stronger in the apples.

Dan Scarborough, Nebraska Cornhusker Alumni

Strip and Go Naked

30 (12 fluid oz) cans or bottles of favorite light beer 1¾ L vodka 2 (12-oz) cans frozen lemonade concentrate, thawed	In a 4- to 5-gallon sports drink dispenser, combine the light beer, vodka, and lemonade concentrate. Stir gently to disperse the lemonade. Put the lid on and serve. Makes 3½ gallons. This party-sized version of the classic vodka, beer, and lemonade cocktail is recommended to consume before a Nebraska football game.

Dan Scarborough, Nebraska Cornhusker Alumni

Nevada

Comstock Lode Miner's Calico Beans

1 lb lean ground beef
½ c chopped purple or yellow onion
½ - 1 lb smoked sliced bacon (cut in 2-inch squares)
2 cans pork and beans
1 can butter beans or lima beans (drained)
1 can kidney beans (drained)
½ c ketchup
⅓ c red vinegar
2 – 3 cloves chopped fresh garlic (or garlic powder)
¼ c brown sugar
1 t Italian seasoning
¼ t dry mustard seasoning (or a T regular mustard)
¼ t cumin seasoning
dash ground black pepper
dash salt
dash Tabasco Sauce (optional, to add "zip")

Over medium-low heat, fully brown the ground beef and onion in a large, non-stick skillet or soup pot. Drain and discard any excess liquid. Set cooked beef aside in a small bowl. Cook the bacon pieces in the same skillet over low heat, pouring off excess grease, but leaving a small amount of oil for flavoring. Bacon should be cooked, but not overly crisp. Add cooked beef back into the skillet with bacon pieces. Add all the remaining beans, spices, brown sugar, ketchup, and vinegar into the skillet and bring mixture to a slow low boil for 5 minutes, stirring gently to combine flavors. Add a dash of Tabasco if a spicier flavor is desired. Cover and continue to simmer on low for 10 to 20 minutes, stirring as needed. Don't overcook. Serve with homemade rolls or corn bread. Note: This recipe can be adapted to your personal preferences. It is not rocket science – just a tasty concoction that sticks to your ribs.

Pam Sessions, a Soldiers' Angel in Nevada

Deluxe Sugar Cookies

1 c butter 1 egg 1½ c powdered sugar ½ t almond extract 1 t vanilla 1 t baking soda 2½ c all-purpose flour 1 t cream of tartar granulated or colored sugar for decorating	Mix butter, powdered sugar, egg, vanilla, and almond extract thoroughly. Blend mixture with the flour, baking soda, and cream of tartar. Cover and chill dough for at least 2 to 3 hours. Preheat oven to 375. Divide dough in half. Roll each half 3/16 inch thick on lightly floured, cloth-covered board. Cut cookies into desired shapes. Sprinkle with granulated sugar or colored sugar. Place on lightly greased baking sheet. Bake 7 to 8 minutes until light brown – don't overbake. Cooled cookies should be stored in airtight container in fridge or frozen. Can also be frosted with vanilla icing and decorated as desired. Variation: Paintbrush Cookies – Before baking, paint cookies with cookie paint with small paintbrush. Bake as usual. Cookie Paint: 1 egg yolk plus ¼ teaspoon water, divided up into several small cups. Add food coloring to make the paint color you wish.

Pam Sessions, a Soldiers' Angel in Nevada

Indian Chili Mac

elbow macaroni 2 cans favorite chili 1 can diced tomatoes or tomato soup 1 can corn, drained (optional) tortilla chips, for serving sour cream, for serving grated cheese, for serving	Cook pasta and drain. Add chili, tomatoes or soup, and corn, if using. Heat thoroughly. Top each serving with chips, sour cream, and cheese.

Patt Sprague, a Soldiers' Angel in Las Vegas, Nevada

Silver State Potatoes

4 medium potatoes, boiled, peeled, and
  grated
2 c sour cream
1 T salt
¼ c milk
¼ c butter
1 can cream of chicken soup
½ c grated Cheddar cheese
½ c chopped onion
corn flakes
softened butter

Combine all ingredients, except potatoes, cornflakes, and softened butter. Simmer on low heat until cheese melts. Add potatoes. Place in lightly greased baking dish. Top with crushed cornflakes mixed with softened butter. Bake at 350 for about 1 hour or until golden brown. Dish freezes and reheats very well.

Bob Miller, Former Governor of Nevada

133

New Hampshire

Apple Crisp

4 c sliced, pared tart apples (about 4 medium-sized apples)
⅔ - ¾ cup brown sugar depending on your sweet tooth (packed)
½ c all-purpose flour
½ c oats
¾ t cinnamon
¾ t nutmeg
⅓ c softened butter
light cream or ice cream, for serving

Heat the oven to 375. Grease a square pan, 8 x 8 x 2 inch pan. Place apple slices in pan. Mix remaining ingredients thoroughly. Sprinkle this over the apples. Bake 30 minutes or until apples are tender and topping is golden brown. Serve warm with light cream or ice cream.

Teri Moore, a Soldiers' Angel in Salem, New Hampshire.

Indian Pudding

6 c milk
½ c unsalted butter
½ c yellow cornmeal
¼ c flour
1 t salt
½ c molasses
3 eggs, beaten
⅓ c granulated sugar
1 t cinnamon
1 t nutmeg
good-quality vanilla ice cream, for serving

Scald the milk and butter in a large double boiler and once it boils, turn the heat to medium. Preheat oven to 250. In another bowl, mix cornmeal, flour, and salt. Stir in molasses and then slowly thin the mixture with ½ cup of scalded milk. Gradually add the mixture back into the large pot of scalded milk on the stove. Cook, stirring mixture until thickened. While constantly whisking, slowly add ½ cup of the hot mixture to the beaten eggs in a bowl. Add this mixture back into the pan on the stove combining them. Stir in sugar and spices until smooth. Now, if you find the mixture to be lumpy, you can run it through a blender to make it smooth or pour small amounts of the mixture into a hand held strainer over the pan and using a spatula force it through the strainer. Pour the entire mixture into a shallow 2½-quart casserole dish. Bake for 2 hours at 250. Allow pudding to cool for about an hour. Reheat it before serving. Serve with a generous dollop of good vanilla ice cream. This is a 'feel good' comfort dessert which is worth the work. Enjoy!

Teri Moore, a Soldiers' Angel in Salem, New Hampshire.

Maple-cured Salmon

1 lb skin-on salmon filet ½ t fresh ground white peppercorns or crushed pink peppercorn freshly grated lemon rind ¾ t maple syrup ¾ t sea salt ⅛ c coarsely chopped dill 1 T chopped fennel tops, leafy part only 1 T good-quality vodka or gin 1 box of specialty crackers, for serving	Place salmon, skin side down on a piece of plastic wrap large enough to snugly wrap the filet in. Mix peppercorns, lemon rind, syrup, and salt together and rub on salmon filet. Toss dill and fennel tops together and place on the salmon. Drizzle vodka or gin over top. Wrap the salmon tightly in the plastic wrap so juices won't escape. Place on a large plate in the refrigerator for 36 hours. Turn the salmon once every 9 hours times during the curing process. Unwrap the salmon and brush off herb/salt mixture. Slice the cured salmon thinly. It is now ready to be eaten on crackers as an appetizer, added to a salad for a hearty lunch, or even added to eggs for a lovely brunch! Enjoy!

Teri Moore, a Soldiers' Angel in Salem, New Hampshire.

New England Clam Chowder

¼ lb salt pork, diced 3 onions, peeled and chopped 1½ qt clam stock and 2 c water, or 2 c bottled clam juice and 1½ qt water 6 potatoes, peeled and cubed 1 t chopped thyme 2 c half-and-half 2 c shucked clams, coarsely chopped salt and pepper to taste	Fry salt pork in soup kettle until crisp. Remove with slotted spoon and set aside. Sauté the onions in fat until tender. Add stock, water, potatoes, and thyme. Simmer, partially covered, 15 minutes or until potatoes are just tender. Add half-and-half, clams, and reserved salt pork. Heat slowly. Do not boil. It is very tasty and great in a mug if you want to have it in the afternoon with a sandwich. Hearty and great comfort food.

Mother, a Soldiers' Angel in Salem, New Hampshire

New Jersey

Homemade Mac and Cheese

1 lb elbow macaroni 1 lb processed cheese (ie, Velveeta), sliced 1 can Cheddar cheese soup 2 soup cans milk 1 stick butter, softened 1 egg 2 T minced onion flakes ½ t pepper breadcrumbs and paprika for topping	Cook elbow macaroni in boiling salted water per package directions. Drain and rinse in cold water. Layer half the macaroni in a baking dish. Layer half the cheese slices over macaroni. Repeat with remaining macaroni and cheese. In a blender, combine cheddar cheese soup and milk. Add egg, butter, onion flakes, and pepper. Blend well and pour over layered macaroni and cheese. Sprinkle breadcrumbs over top and a little paprika. Bake at 350 for 45 minutes.

Princess Leah, a Soldiers' Angel in New Jersey

Jersey Fresh Cranberry Muffins

2 c flour 1 c sugar 1½ t baking powder ½ t baking soda 1 t salt ¼ c butter 1 beaten egg 1 t grated orange rind ¾ c orange juice 2 c chopped cranberries	In a blender, mix dry ingredients. With 2 knives or pastry blender cut in butter. Add egg, orange juice, rind, and berries. Mix until just combined. Grease muffin tins and bake at 350 until golden brown.

Anne Hartley, a Soldiers' Angel in Texas

New Mexico

Bizcochitos

2 c lard (can also use vegetable shortening but not as good) 1½ c sugar 2 eggs 2 t anise seeds, toasted 6 c all-purpose flour 3 t baking powder 1 t salt ½ c brandy (can also use a dry burgundy wine) sugar and cinnamon	Preheat oven to 350. Cream lard or shortening. Add sugar, eggs, and anise seeds; cream again. Mix dry ingredients separately and combine with shortening mixture. Add brandy or wine as needed and mix thoroughly. Roll out dough on a floured surface and cut into shapes. Bake for 12 to 15 minutes until lightly browned. While still hot, cover in sugar and cinnamon mixture.

Cara Gregory (Scooterjoey), a Soldiers' Angel in New Mexico

Black-eyed Pea Salad

2 (15.5-oz) cans black-eyed peas 2 c Italian dressing 2 c chopped green pepper 1½ c diced white onion 1 c finely chopped green onions ½ c finely chopped jalapeno peppers 1 T chopped garlic salt to taste hot pepper sauce to taste	Mix all ingredients. Marinate overnight in the refrigerator.

Sammye Pruett, a Soldiers' Angel in Hobbs, New Mexico

Cabbage Salad

1 (12-oz) pkg broccoli slaw 1 c slivered almonds (toasted is better) 1 c sunflower seeds 2 (2.8-oz) pkg oriental flavor ramen noodles ¼ c red wine vinegar ¾ c oil ½ c sugar	Crush noodles and set flavor packets aside. Bring to boil, red wine vinegar, oil, sugar, and the 2 packets of oriental flavoring from the noodle packages. Mix slaw, almonds, sunflower seeds, and crushed noodles. Pour hot liquid over slaw mixture. Mix well and refrigerate overnight. Recipe makes a lot and can be cut in half.

Ruth Ann Pruett, Hobbs, New Mexico

Layered Chicken Enchiladas

½ c cooking oil 8 corn tortillas 2 c (8 oz) shredded Monterey Jack cheese 1 c shredded or cubed cooked chicken 1 (4.5-oz.) can chopped green chilies ¼ c chopped onion 1 (10-oz) can green chilies enchilada sauce 1 can evaporated milk	Preheat oven to 350. In small skillet, heat oil to 350. Dip each tortilla in hot oil for 2 to 3 seconds to soften; drain on paper towels. Place tortilla on lightly greased baking sheet. Top with 1/4 cup cheese, 1/4 cup chicken, 1 1/2 tablespoons green chilies and 1 tablespoon onion. Top with a second tortilla; pour 1/3 cup enchilada sauce mixed with evaporated milk over top. Sprinkle with 1/4 cup cheese. Repeat with remaining tortillas to make 4 stacks. Bake 15 minutes.

Jean, a Soldiers' Angel in New Mexico

Mexican Corn Bread

1 c flour 2 t baking powder 1 egg ¼ c melted margarine ½ c grated cheese 2 green chilies, chopped ¾ c corn meal ½ t salt ¾ c milk ½ c drained canned corn 2 T diced onion	Preheat oven to 400. Mix dry ingredients; add egg, milk, and margarine. Stir until blended. Stir in corn, onion, green chili, and cheese. Pour into greased and lightly dusted (with corn meal) 8 x 8 inch baking pan. Bake 25 minutes.

Jean, a Soldiers' Angel in New Mexico

Mexican Fries

1 lb pkg frozen French fries 1 T cooking oil 1 t chili powder seasoning 1 t seasoned salt ¼ t oregano ¼ t garlic powder ¼ t ground cumin	Mix oil and seasoning. Add fries and toss with seasoning mixture until mixed well. Bake at 450 for approximately 30 minutes

Jean, a Soldiers' Angel in New Mexico

Red Chile Pork

2 T New Mexico red chili powder ½ lb lean pork, chopped 1 clove garlic 1 T flour ½ c water cumin to taste salt to taste	Mix all ingredients in large saucepan, bring to a boil, and simmer to consistency of your liking.

ddhalely, a Soldiers' Angel in New Mexico

New York

Buffalo Chicken Wing Dip

3 c cooked chicken, shredded ⅔ c wing sauce (or hot sauce) 2 (8-oz) pkg cream cheese, softened ⅓ c blue cheese dressing 1 c shredded Cheddar cheese, divided celery sticks or tortilla chips, for serving	Mix chicken, wing sauce, cream cheese, blue cheese, and ½ cup of shredded cheddar. Spread in a baking dish (roughly 9 inch round). Top with remaining ½ cup shredded cheddar. Bake at 350 for 30 minutes or until bubbly. Serve with celery or tortilla chips.

Alicia Bell, a Soldiers' Angel in Marion, New York

Croghan Bologna

2 lb ground beef 1½ T Morton's tender quick ½ T garlic powder ½ t onion powder 1 c water 2 T liquid smoke	Mix all ingredients well and let stand in refrigerator for 24 hours. Roll in aluminum foil to measure 2 inch by 8 inch; seal ends well. Bake at 300 on cookie sheet for about 1 hour 15 minutes. Let cool. Serve with your favorite cheese and crackers. Can also be served with yellow mustard.

Alicia Bell, a Soldiers' Angel in Marion, New York

Lemon Chicken

thin sliced chicken breasts (approximately pkg of 4 - 6 or more if you like) 1 c flour salt and pepper to taste paprika ½ t basil, dried or finely chopped fresh 1 T chopped garlic (I use chopped garlic in olive oil from a jar) 2 T butter 1 lemon, sliced ½ c white wine	Combine flour, salt, pepper, and paprika, in zip lock bag. Coat chicken in bag; shake off excess flour. Melt butter in pan, add chicken, and brown lightly. Remove to plate. Add garlic, basil, and white wine to pan and let simmer for 1 minute. Return chicken to pan, top with lemon slices, cover and simmer for 2 to 3 minutes. This recipe is easy to adjust for smaller or larger servings.

Diane Fairben, a Soldiers' Angel in New York

Mamma Jen's Carne Molida

1 – 2 cloves garlic 1 lb Monterey jack cheese, shredded 1½ lb ground beef 1 green bell pepper 1 large yellow onion 2 small cans tomato sauce 1 small bag of Yukon gold or russet potatoes	In a deep fry pan, brown hamburger meat with salt, pepper, and half of onion and 1 glove of garlic until cooked. Drain fat. Peel potatoes and quarter them, then slice them about a quarter inch thick, Add to meat. Slice green pepper into long strips. Do the same with remaining onion and add both to the meat. Add the tomato sauce with 2 cans of water until potatoes are covered just over the top layer to cook the potatoes. Let simmer on low for 45 minutes or until potatoes are done. The mixture should be thick and stew like. Grate cheese. Take bowls and put the Monterey jack on the bottom and add the stew to it. I make burritos out of it with large flour tortillas. Great on a cold day or tight budget; will feed up to 6 or 8 people… just add more ingredients to feed more people.

Jennifer Miller-Bauer, a Soldiers' Angel in Rochester, New York

New York Cheesecake

2 c sour cream 1 lb ricotta cheese ½ c butter, melted 1½ c sugar 16 oz cream cheese 3 T flour 3 extra-large eggs 5 T vanilla 3 T cornstarch 5 T lemon juice	Combine sour cream and ricotta cheese in a large mixing bowl. Beating at low speed, add butter, sugar and cream cheese. Increase speed to medium and add flour, eggs, vanilla, cornstarch, and lemon juice. Beat for 5 minutes. Pour into springform pan. Bake in preheated 350 oven for 1 hour, then turn off oven and leave in closed oven for 1 hour longer. Cool on rack. This cheesecake has no crust.

Patt, a Soldiers' Angel from New York

New York City Black and White Cookies

1 c all-purpose flour ⅔ c cake flour, not self-rising ½ t baking powder ¼ t salt 2 large eggs ¾ c granulated sugar ½ c milk 6 T unsalted butter, melted and cooled ½ t pure vanilla extract ½ t pure lemon extract 2 c confectioners' sugar, sifted 2 T light corn syrup, plus more if needed 1½ oz bittersweet chocolate, melted	Preheat oven to 350. Sift together flours, baking powder, and salt; set aside. In a medium bowl, whisk eggs and sugar until smooth. Add milk, and whisk to combine. Whisk in melted butter and extracts. Add flour mixture, and stir to form a smooth dough. Cover, and chill for 1 hour. Line baking pans with Silpat nonstick baking mats. Using a 2-ounce scoop, drop 5 cookies per pan, 3 inches apart. Bake until edges are light brown, 12 to 15 minutes. Transfer cookies to a wire rack set over parchment paper to cool. In a small bowl, combine confectioners' sugar, 3 tablespoons hot water, and corn syrup. Whisk until smooth. Using a small offset spatula, ice half of each cookie. Return cookies to rack to drip, if necessary. Add chocolate to remaining icing. Stir until smooth. Add additional corn syrup to thin to desired consistency, if necessary. Spread chocolate icing over second half of each cookie. Allow cookies to set, about 10 minutes.

Ginger Grant, a Soldiers' Angel in Brooklyn, New York

Winter Survival Pizza	
1 pkg pizza crust mix ½ c Parmesan cheese (or any cheese) 1 jar pizza sauce (or ½ jar pasta sauce) any suitable perishable food left in your refrigerator	Heat wood stove (or kerosene heater; have also heard a grill works) as hot as possible. Mix dough according to directions. Grease 2 metal pie plates and spread the dough. Spread sauce evenly. Top with cheese and toppings. Put aluminum foil over the top and place on wood stove. Cook until crust is browned on bottom.

Alicia Bell, a Soldiers' Angel in Marion, New York

North Carolina

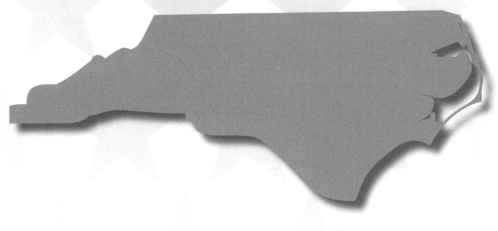

Amazing German Chocolate Cake

vegetable oil spray for misting the pan flour for dusting the pan 1 pkg German chocolate cake mix 1 (15-oz) can coconut pecan frosting 1 c water ⅓ c vegetable oil 3 large eggs	Place rack in center of oven and preheat to 350. Lightly mist a 12-cup Bundt pan with vegetable oil spray, then dust with flour. Shake out excess flour. Set pan aside. Place cake mix, frosting, water, oil, and eggs in a large mixing bowl. Blend with mixer on low speed for 1 minute. Stop and scrape down the sides of the bowl with a spatula. Increase mixer speed to medium and beat 2 minutes. The batter should look thick and well combined. Pour the batter into the prepared pan, smoothing it out with spatula. Place the pan in oven. Bake until cake springs back when lightly pressed with your finger, 45 to 50 minutes. Remove pan from oven and place on wire rack to cool for 20 minutes. Invert onto wire rack to cool completely. Slide cake onto serving platter. Slice and serve. Store this cake in a cake saver or under a glass dome at room temperature for up to 1 week. Also freezes well. Thaw overnight in refrigerator before serving.

Betty C Watson, a Soldiers' Angel in North Carolina

Aunt Bee's Bingo Cherry Salad

2 (3-oz) pkg cherry gelatin 2 c boiling water 1 (20-oz) can crushed pineapple 1 (21-oz) can cherry pie filling 1 (8-oz) pkg cream cheese ½ c sugar ½ c sour cream 1 t vanilla extract ½ c chopped pecans	In a large bowl, combine the gelatin and hot water. Add the pineapple and cherry pie filling. Pour into an 8 x 10 inch glass dish. Chill until set. Soften the cream cheese and mix well with the sugar. Blend in the sour cream and vanilla. Spread over the gelatin mixture. Sprinkle with nuts.

Christine Distelhorst, a Soldiers' Angel in Greensboro, North Carolina

Beef Stroganoff

1½ lb round steak ¼ c flour 2 t salt dash of pepper 2 T butter 1 lb fresh mushrooms 2 T ketchup 1 c beef consommé 1 T Worcestershire sauce 1 t dry mustard ½ c sour cream hot rice or egg noodles, for serving	Cut round steak into 4 pieces. Place on waxed paper or board and pound flour mixed with salt and pepper into it with a mallet or the edge of a heavy saucer. Cut meat into ½-inch strips. Melt butter in heavy skillet; brown meat. Add all other ingredients except the sour cream. Simmer slowly until the meat is tender, adding more consommé if necessary. Cook about 1 hour. If desired, bring to table in chafing dish. Just before serving, stir in sour cream. Heat but do not boil. Serve with noodles or rice.

Judi Brinegar, a Soldiers' Angel in North Carolina

Chicken and Fruit Salad

4 large chicken breasts seedless grapes pineapple chunks, drained but reserve juice pecans dash celery salt black pepper ranch dressing lettuce and melba toast, for serving	Cook chicken breasts until done. Dice chicken into cubes. Add seedless grapes, pineapple chunks, pecans, dash of celery salt, and black pepper. Mix with a little bit of ranch dressing mixed with pineapple juice. Serve over a bed of lettuce and serve with melba toast.

Laura, a Soldiers' Angel in North Carolina

Heavenly Cream Squares

1¼ c vanilla wafer crumbs
½ c chopped pecans
½ c melted margarine (Parkay is called for)
1 pkg vanilla pudding (cooked type)
¼ t imitation rum flavoring
1 (8-oz) pkg cream cheese

Combine crumbs, pecans, and margarine, reserving 1/2 cup of mixture for topping. Press onto the bottom of a 9-inch square pan. Prepare pudding according to directions on package. Remove from heat and add cream cheese, stirring until blended. Add rum flavoring and mix thoroughly. Pour into crumb-lined pan. Sprinkle with the remaining crumb mixture. Chill. When ready to serve, cut into squares.

Brenda L Wayne, a Soldiers' Angel in Gastonia, North Carolina

Jewels and Stars Bars

1 (10-oz) bag white vanilla baking chips
½ c butter or margarine
1¼ c plain flour
¾ c sugar
1 t vanilla
¼ t salt
3 eggs
1 (16-oz) container vanilla frosting
½ c small gumdrops

Heat oven to 350. Grease bottom and sides of 13 x 9-inch pan with shortening and lightly flour. In a heavy 2-qt saucepan, heat baking chips and butter over low heat, stirring frequently, until just melted. Mixture may appear curdled. Remove from heat, cool. Stir in flour, sugar, vanilla, salt, and eggs. Pour into pan. Bake 24 to 27 minutes or until toothpick inserted in the center comes out clean. Cool completely on wire rack, about 1 hour. Spread with frosting. Flatten some gumdrops with bottom of heavy drinking glass. Cut with star-shaped cutter. Place gumdrop stars on regular gumdrops (the jewels) on frosting. Cut into 8 by 4 rows to make bars.

Judi Brinegar, a Soldiers' Angel in North Carolina

Pineapple Au Gratin

2 c Cheddar cheese, grated 1 c sugar 2 cans pineapple chunks, drained 6 T self-rising flour 1 sleeve crackers 1 stick butter, melted	Mix all ingredients and put into a baking dish. Crush crackers and mix with butter. Put on top of pineapple. Bake at 350 for 30 minutes.

Angie Rohrer, a Soldiers' Angel in Kernersville, North Carolina

Slow Cooker Pulled Pork, Eastern North Carolina Style

4 - 5 lb bone-in pork shoulder salt and pepper to taste 1½ - 2 c cider vinegar 2 - 3 T brown sugar 2 t ground cayenne pepper 2 t crushed red pepper flakes hot pepper sauce to taste	Season pork shoulder with salt and pepper, then place into slow cooker. Pour vinegar around the pork, and cover. Cook on low setting for 12 hours, by which time the pork should pull apart easily. Remove the pork from slow cooker, and discard bones. Strain the liquid, reserving 2 cups. Shred the pork using 2 forks, and return it to slow cooker. Stir brown sugar, cayenne pepper, red pepper flakes, and hot pepper sauce into the reserved liquid, and then add it to the pot and mix into pork. Cover pot and set on warm until served.

Barbara Bergan, a Soldiers' Angel in Leland, North Carolina

Stuffed Peppers with Beef

4 green peppers 1 lb ground beef, uncooked 1 egg 1 chopped onion salt and pepper	Cut off stem ends and remove seeds from green peppers, boil 2 minutes, drain. Mix meat with egg, onion, and seasonings. Fill peppers with meat mixture. Place in pan, add a little water, cover pan, and simmer on top of range or in a moderate oven (350), about 30 minutes.

Judi Brinegar, a Soldiers' Angel in North Carolina

Sweet Potato Casserole

2 lb sweet potatoes ¼ c sugar or maple syrup ¼ c butter ½ t salt 1 c marshmallows 1 small can of crushed pineapple ¼ c pecan pieces	Boil potatoes until tender and peel. Mash, add sugar or syrup, butter, and salt, and mix well. Turn into greased baking dish, top with marshmallows and pineapple. Place in moderate oven of 350, until brown. Serve hot.

Judi Brinegar, a Soldiers' Angel in North Carolina

North Dakota

Buffaloaf

2 lbs ground bison salt and pepper 1 medium onion, chopped garlic salt ¼ c green olives, chopped ½ c ketchup 2 t Worcestershire sauce	Mix all ingredients except ketchup, and form into loaf. Pour ketchup over top of loaf. Bake at 275 to 300 for approximately 1 hour. Serve on platter with desired garnishes.

Emmaleis McPherron, a Soldiers' Angel in North Dakota

Buffalo Bacon Wrapped Shrimp

1 lb (21 – 24 per lb) shrimp, uncooked, peeled, and deveined ¼ lb bison bacon, cut into ½ inch wide x 2 inch long strips ¼ c olive oil 2 T soy sauce 1 T sherry vinegar ¼ c Thai sweet chili sauce (I use Mae Ploy brand) juice and zest of 1 orange 1 T minced garlic ¼ t red pepper flakes ¼ c seedless raspberry jam chopped fresh parsley tooth picks or kebab skewers, soaked in water if using bamboo ones	Wisk together olive oil, soy sauce, vinegar, chili sauce, juice and zest, garlic, and pepper flakes. Toss in shrimp coating evenly. Marinade for at least 1 hour, however no more than 3. Wrap each shrimp around the middle with a strip of bison bacon and either skewer with a tooth pick (if using a grilling pan) or kebab skewer if using the grill (preferable method; toss in some mesquite chips, too, for extra flavor). Grill for approximately 5 minutes on the first side and 3 on the second side. Remove from the grill or grill pan and while the shrimp are resting, melt the raspberry jam in the microwave for approximately 50 to 60 seconds and, with a spoon, drizzle over the shrimp and sprinkle with the parsley for garnish. Serve immediately and enjoy!

Jen Skibicki, a Soldiers' Angel in North Dakota

Buffalo Meatballs

2 lb ground bison burger 2 eggs, beaten 1 c bread crumbs 1 pkg onion soup mix 1 can sauerkraut (large; rinsed once) 1 jar chili sauce 1 can whole cranberries in cranberry jelly 1 c brown sugar	Preheat oven to 350. Mix bison, eggs, bread crumbs, and soup mix; roll into bite-size meatballs. Place in 9 x 12 inch pan, set aside. Mix sauerkraut, chili sauce, cranberries, and brown sugar. Pour over meatballs. Bake 1½ hours stirring once after 1 hour and again when done. Serve warm on toothpicks.

Shelle Michaels, National Communications Officer, Ladies of Liberty Director, and State of North Dakota Director

Buffalo Wheels

1 (8-oz.) pkg cream cheese 2 t hot sauce ⅓ c sour cream 8 large pimento stuffed olives, chopped 2 T finely chopped parsley 2 T hot peppers, chopped 1 T crushed garlic 1 lb bison pastrami 1 t lemon pepper 12 (8-inch) flour tortilla wraps	Combine cream cheese, hot sauce, sour cream, olives, parsley, hot peppers, lemon pepper, and garlic in a bowl and mix well. Spread a thin layer of the cream cheese mixture over a flour tortilla. Then, place a thin layer of the pastrami over the top of the cream cheese mixture. Roll up tightly and secure with toothpicks if necessary. Then repeat with the remaining cream cheese mixture and tortillas. Cover and refrigerate until ready to serve. Remove toothpicks and cut into 3/4 inch slices. Makes 4 to 5 dozen.

Rebbekah McPherron, a Soldiers' Angel in North Dakota

Cookie Salad

1 c buttermilk 1 small package vanilla instant pudding 1 can drained Mandarin oranges 1 can pineapple chunks with juice 8 oz frozen whipped topping, thawed fudge stripe cookies, crushed	Mix buttermilk and pudding. Add oranges, pineapple chunks with juice, whipped topping, and crushed cookies. Place in fridge 2 hours to set.

Stephanie Johnson, a Soldiers' Angel in Luverne, North Dakota

Grandma Beezie's Carrot Cake with Cream Cheese Frosting

½ c butter or shortening 1 c packed brown sugar 2 eggs 1 t vanilla ¾ c carrot puree 1 t cinnamon ¼ t ginger ¼ t nutmeg 1 c flour ½ t soda ½ c nuts (optional) ½ t salt 8 oz cream cheese softened 1 stick butter, softened 2½ - 3 c powdered sugar	Cream butter and sugar. Add eggs, vanilla, carrot puree, cinnamon, ginger, and nutmeg. Mix flour, soda, salt, and nuts and add to creamed mixture. Bake in 9 x 13 pan for 25 to 30 min at 350. For frosting, mix cream cheese, butter, and powdered sugar to make frosting thick enough to spread on cooled cake.

Stephanie Johnson, a Soldiers' Angel in Luverne, North Dakota

Juneberry Pie

pastry for a 2-crust pie, 9 inch 4 c Juneberries ⅓ c flour 1½ c sugar ¼ t nutmeg 1 t cinnamon 1 T vinegar 1½ T butter	Wash berries thoroughly, draining well. Mix flour, sugar, and cinnamon. Fold into the berries. Add vinegar and put into pie crust. Dot with butter. Cover with top crust, slit or make lattice if preferred. Bake at 375 or 35 minutes or until browned and juice bubbles through the slits. Serve slightly warm.

Shelle Michaels, National Communications Officer, Ladies of Liberty Director, and State of North Dakota Director

Norwegian Butter Cookies

½ c butter 2 eggs ¼ c white sugar 1 c all-purpose flour ½ t vanilla extract	Preheat oven to 375. Hard boil the eggs and separate the yolks. Cream the butter and hard-boiled egg yolks. Beat in the sugar and add the flour and vanilla extract. Mix thoroughly. Put through a cookie press or arrange by teaspoonfuls on ungreased cookie sheets. Bake 10 to 12 minutes, or until lightly browned.

Shelle Michaels, National Communications Officer, Ladies of Liberty Director, and State of North Dakota Director

Rhubarb Crisp

6 c fine-cut rhubarb sugar (optional) 1½ c oatmeal 1½ c flour 1½ c brown sugar ¾ c melted butter ½ t baking powder	Put rhubarb in a greased 9 x 13 inch; sprinkle with sugar if desired (my family likes the rhubarb tart). Mix oatmeal, flour, sugar, butter, and baking powder. Put on top of rhubarb. Bake for 35 to 45 minutes at 350.

Stephanie Johnson, a Soldiers' Angel in Luverne, North Dakota

Ohio

Ashtabula Picnic Salad	
2 - 4 medium-to-large tomatoes 1 - 2 medium-to-large cucumbers 8 - 16 oz block of mozzarella cheese black pepper dried basil leaves oil and vinegar salad dressing (I use Newman's Own Olive Oil and Vinegar)	Slice tomatoes no more than ¼ inch thick and line bottom of serving tray or glass dish with single layer as you slice. Stop slicing tomatoes when bottom of dish is covered. Slices will hold up better if you slice the tomatoes vertically (parallel with stem) rather than horizontally. Slice mozzarella slightly less than ¼ inch thick and place a slice or half slice on top of each tomato to fit across tomato slice without hanging over the edge. Slice cucumber ⅛ to ¼ inch thick and place one on top of each mozzarella slice. Drizzle (do not drench or soak) oil and vinegar dressing over stacks of tomatoes, mozzarella, and cucumber. Sprinkle with black pepper and basil to taste. Two medium stacks of tomato, mozzarella, and cucumber usually make one serving.

Thelma Best, a Soldiers' Angel in Centerville, Ohio

Asiago Cheese Bread

3 c all-purpose flour ¼ t active dry yeast 1¾ t salt ½ - 1 c grated Asiago Cheese cornmeal	In a large bowl, combine flour, yeast, salt, and cheese. Add 1½ cups plus 2 tablespoons water. Stir until blended. The dough will be shaggy and very sticky. Cover the bowl with plastic wrap. Let the dough rest at warm room temperature until the surface is dotted with bubbles, 12 to 18 hours. (It depends on the temperature in your house.) Place the dough on a lightly floured work surface. Sprinkle the dough with a little flour and fold the dough over onto itself once or twice. Cover loosely with plastic wrap and let rest for 15 minutes. Using just enough flour to keep the dough from sticking to the work surface or your fingers, gently and quickly shape the dough into a ball. Generously coat a cotton towel, preferably a flour sack towel (not terry cloth) with cornmeal. Put the dough, seam side down on the towel and dust with more cornmeal. Cover with another cotton towel and let rise until the dough is more than double in size and does not readily spring back when poked with a finger, about 2 hours. At least 30 minutes before the dough is ready, put a 2 ¾ quart enameled cast iron pot with lid on into the oven and preheat the oven to 450. Carefully remove the pot from the oven. Slide your hand under the towel and turn the dough over, seam side up, into the pot. It may look like a mess, but that's OK. Shake the pan once or twice if the dough is unevenly distributed: it will straighten out as it bakes. Cover with lid and bake for 30 minutes. Uncover and continue baking until the loaf is browned, 15 to 30 minutes more. Check at 15 minute time. Transfer the pot to a wire rack and let cool for 10 minutes. Using oven mitts, turn the pot on its side and gently turn the bread; it will release easily.

Sharon Smith, a Soldiers' Angel in Westlake, Ohio

Buckeyes

1 c creamy peanut butter 4 oz plus 3 T softened butter 1 t vanilla extract 3½ - 4 c confectioners sugar ½ c very fine graham cracker crumbs 3 c semisweet chocolate chips	With a wooden spoon or large mixer with paddle attachment, beat peanut butter, butter, and vanilla until smooth. Slowly stir or beat in confectioners' sugar and graham cracker crumbs. Mixture will be dry, but will hold together when shaped into balls. Shape mixture into 1-inch balls; place on wax paper-lined cookie sheet and chill in freezer or until firm. Melt chocolate chips over hot water. Spear a peanut butter ball with toothpick or dipping fork and dip ball into the chocolate to cover most of it. Place chocolate side down on cookie sheet. If desired, leave the top uncovered to resemble the Ohio buckeye nuts. If desired, drizzle more butter over the balls to fill in gaps made by toothpick or dipping fork. Refrigerate buckeyes for about 2 hours or longer, or until the chocolate is set. Store buckeyes tightly covered in refrigerator or freezer. Makes about 5 dozen buckeye candies.

Betty Gregovich, a Soldiers' Angel in North Olmsted, Ohio

Cincinnati 3-Way Chili

1 qt hot water 2 lb ground beef 1 (12-oz) can tomato paste 1 large onion, chopped 3 T chili powder 3 bay leaves 1 T salt 1 t ground cinnamon 1 t ground black pepper 1 t ground allspice 1 t white wine vinegar ½ t ground cumin ½ t Worcestershire sauce ¼ t ground cayenne pepper ¼ t garlic powder 1 lb spaghetti noodles, freshly cooked 1 c grated Cheddar cheese Tabasco sauce (optional) oyster crackers (optional)	Pour water into large saucepan or Dutch oven. Crumble in beef. Add next 13 ingredients. Simmer 3 hours, stirring occasionally. Discard bay leaves. Pour cooked spaghetti into serving platter or large pasta bowl. Pour chili over spaghetti. Top with cheese. Add Tabasco sauce to taste if desired or serve as condiment. Serve immediately with oyster crackers on the side. 4-way chili: add 2 (15 oz) cans pinto beans, drained and rinsed, to 3-way beef mixture to simmer. 5-way chili: add raw onions to 4-way before topping with cheese.

Thelma Best, a Soldiers' Angel in Centerville, Ohio

Ohio Farmer Spinach and Spaghetti Dish

2 lb fresh spinach (washed and cut) 1 beaten egg 1 c sour cream ½ c milk 1 c Parmesan cheese 2 t minced onion (farmer recommended fresh) dash of salt and pepper paprika (optional) 2 c shredded farmer's cheese (or Monterey jack) 3 c cooked and drained spaghetti (my short-cut; the farmer made his own egg noodles)	Combine all ingredients, mix well and pour into ungreased glass cake pan; sprinkle with Parmesan cheese and paprika, if desired. Bake covered for 20 minutes at 350, then uncover and bake 15 minutes at 300.

I Willis, a Soldiers' Angel in Ohio

Pumpkin Muffins

1 box spice cake mix 1 c pumpkin 2 eggs ⅔ c water ½ bag chocolate chips (regular or I like to use Special Dark)	Mix all ingredients, bake in minimuffin tins at 350 for 12 to 15 minutes. Super easy, but always a big hit.

Kelley Sral, a Soldiers' Angel in Wooster, Ohio

Strawberry Pie with Rhubarb (Husband's Grandmother's Recipe)

2 lb strawberries (washed and cut in half) 2 c rhubarb (fresh/ frozen), washed and cut 1 c sugar pinch of salt pinch nutmeg 3 T tapioca butter frozen pie pastry (of course grandma made her own) whipped cream, for serving	Mix all ingredients (except pastry); let stand 10 minutes, and pour into crust. Dot with butter and top with lattice strips. Bake 40 minutes at 400.

I Willis, a Soldiers' Angel in Ohio

Oklahoma

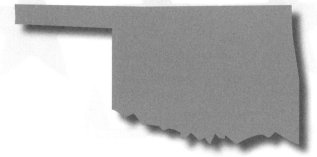

Calf Fry Pâté (Bull Butter)

1 lb calf fries, trimmed and peeled ½ c all-purpose flour ¼ c vegetable oil ½ c finely chopped onion 1 medium Granny Smith apple, peeled and chopped 1 garlic clove, chopped 4 hard-boiled large eggs, coarsely chopped 1 c chicken stock or low-sodium chicken broth ¾ c unsalted butter, softened ½ c shelled natural pistachios, toasted 2 t Dijon mustard ½ t freshly grated nutmeg ¼ t ground cloves 2 t salt, or to taste pinch of cayenne 2 T Cognac 2 T fresh lemon juice sliced baguette or crackers, for serving	First, clean calf fries. Each fry is enclosed in a sac of skin with a small opening. Pull the opening apart with your fingers to reveal the tender, membrane-covered portion inside. Cut the skin away with a knife, leaving the membrane intact. Then proceed with the recipe. Halve calf fries lengthwise with a sharp knife, then pat dry with paper towels. Season flour with salt and pepper and dredge fries to lightly coat, shaking off excess. Heat oil in a 12-inch heavy skillet over moderate heat until hot but not smoking, then sauté fries in 2 batches until golden brown on both sides and cooked through, 2 to 3 minutes. Transfer to paper towels to drain. Purée fries in a food processor with remaining ingredients until smooth and transfer to a serving bowl. Chill, covered, until firm, at least 4 hours. Bring to room temperature before serving. Cooks' note: Bull butter may be chilled up to 4 days. Note: Animal fries, or testicles, have a mild flavor and delicate texture somewhat like sweetbreads. They are considered a seasonal delicacy, usually in the spring. Traditionally they are a treat that hungry cowboys cooked for themselves, usually battered and deep fried but sometimes just cooked over the branding fire. Also, calf fries are from young bulls as only they carry the required equipment. After "donation" the bulls are known as steers. There is no such thing as cow fries as a cow is the female of the bovine species.

Pat Miller, a Soldiers' Angel in Oklahoma

Champagne Salad

1 (8-oz) package cream cheese ¾ c sugar 1 large can pineapple tidbits, drained ½ c pecans (chopped) 1 package frozen strawberries (thawed, save the juice) 2 bananas (sliced) 1 small container frozen whipped topping, thawed	Blend cream cheese and sugar in small bowl. In another large container, combine the drained pineapple tidbits, pecans, strawberries (thawed with juice), and bananas. Fold in whipped topping; fold in the cream cheese and sugar mixture. Cover container, freeze for about 30 minutes before ready to serve.

Tina Kliewer, a Soldiers' Angel in Oklahoma City, Oklahoma

Corn Casserole

1 (No. 2) can cream-style corn 1 T chopped jalapeño (can use pickled slices, finely diced) 1 chopped onion 1 egg ½ c milk ¼ c melted butter 1 c cracker crumbs 1 (No. 2) can whole kernel corn, drained 1 c shredded Cheddar cheese (or any flavor)	Mix all ingredients, except cheese. Place in buttered casserole; sprinkle with shredded cheese. Bake at 350 for 1 hour.

Mary Anne Johnson, a Soldiers' Angel in Weslaco, Texas and Cherrille Mashore, in Lone Grove, Oklahoma

Corn and Squash – Traditional Version (Pawnee Tribe)

12 or more ears of raw corn 1 stick butter (not margarine) ¼ c chopped jalapeño peppers (for each 1 c corn cut from the cob) ½ c yellow and green squash, cut into 1-inch chunks (for every 1 c corn cut from the cob)	Cut the corn off a dozen (or more) ears of raw corn. Place into a large cast iron skillet over medium heat. Add butter, stirring occasionally until the butter is melted and distributed over all the corn. While it is cooking, for every cup of corn, add 1/4 cup of chopped jalapeño and mix well. Then add, for every cup of corn, add ½ cup of yellow and green squash cut into 1-inch chunks. Sauté until the squash is cooked al dente. Serve with grilled pork chops from a home-grown hog, smoked tenderloin, or bbq'd ribs.

Pat Miller, a Soldiers' Angel in Oklahoma

Corn and Squash – Version for People with Diabetes (Pawnee Tribe)

4 T butter or corn oil 1 large yellow onion, chopped 2 medium yellow squash, cubed 1 red bell pepper, roasted, seeded, and chopped 4 c whole kernel yellow sweet corn ½ c parsley, chopped fine salt and pepper to taste ½ c water or chicken stock, if needed	Warm butter or oil in a large frying pan over medium heat. Quickly sauté the onion for 3 to 5 minutes, stirring to cook evenly. Add the squash and chopped pepper, stirring to blend well, and cook for an additional 5 minutes. Stir occasionally to keep mixture from sticking. Add the corn, the remaining seasonings, and liquid, if needed. Blend thoroughly, lower heat, cover, and cook for 10 to 15 minutes, stirring once or twice. Serve hot and enjoy. This zesty vegetable side dish is a perfect complement to roast meat and frybread. A combination of seasonal, colorful peppers may be roasted and added for savory flavor and to turn up the heat, if desired. Note: Roasted and peeled peppers are not only more flavorful, but much more digestible.

Pat Miller, a Soldiers' Angel in Oklahoma

Land Run Sweet Biscuits

2 c flour
1 T baking powder
½ t salt
1 c butter
1 T molasses
⅔ c buttermilk (if you don't have buttermilk, use ⅔ cup whole milk in a glass jar, add ½ t white vinegar to it and shake, and wait 30 minutes for it to turn into buttermilk)
1 c butter pecan syrup
1 c chopped pecans

Preheat oven to 450. Put dry ingredients in a large mixing bowl and mix with your dry hands. Using 2 knives or a large fork, work in the butter and molasses until the mixture is crumbly. Use your fist to make a bowl shape in the middle of the flour mixture, and add the buttermilk. Mix with a large fork until dough begins to stick together, and then knead into a soft ball with your hands, using flour on your hands to prevent sticking. Pinch dough into 1 ½ inch balls, and flatten to ½-inch thick circles. This should make about 15 biscuits. Place the biscuits (not touching) into 2 warm, greased cast iron skillets, and place into a 450 oven for about 8 to 10 minutes. When biscuits are lightly browned on top, remove from oven, and pour syrup over all the biscuits in the pan, then sprinkle on the chopped pecans. Place back in over under the broiler for about a minute to caramelize the syrup and pecans. Serve warm. Note: This is considered to be an authentic 100-year-old recipe.

Pat Miller, a Soldiers' Angel in Oklahoma

Oklahoma Brisket

½ c honey
3 T soy sauce
seasoned salt to taste
1 (5-lb) beef brisket
1 c apple cider
¾ c ketchup (catsup)
¼ c packed brown sugar
2 T Worcestershire sauce
¼ c apple cider vinegar
½ t garlic powder, or to taste

Preheat oven to 300. Season the brisket all over with seasoned salt, and place in a roasting pan. Pour the apple cider over it, and cover tightly with aluminum foil. Roast the brisket for 3 hours in the preheated oven. DON'T PEEK! Prepare a grill for low heat. In a small bowl, stir together the honey and soy sauce, and season with seasoned salt. When the roast comes out of the oven, place it on the preheated grill. Grill for 30 minutes, turning frequently and basting with the honey sauce. Meanwhile, in a saucepan over low heat, make a barbeque sauce by combining the ketchup, brown sugar, Worcestershire sauce, cider vinegar, seasoned salt, and the garlic powder. Cook and stir over low heat for 15 minutes without allowing the sauce to boil. If you boil the sauce, it becomes very vinegary. Let brisket rest for about 10 minutes after it comes off the grill. Slice and serve with the barbeque sauce.

Mary Anne Johnson, a Soldiers' Angel in Weslaco, Texas and Cherrille Mashore, in Lone Grove, Oklahoma

Oregon

Hazelnut Pancakes

3 c buttermilk pancake mix ¼ lb hazelnuts, chopped ¼ t nutmeg ¼ t almond extract 1 t vanilla water as needed	In a food processor or blender, grind hazelnuts into a meal (some small chunks are okay). Mix nuts with 1 cup water and seasonings. Add to mix with more water to proper consistency. Cook as you would any pancake.

Pam W, a Soldiers' Angel in Oregon

Simply Baked Salmon or Trout

3 lb salmon or trout steaks (not fillets) 1 t salt, kosher 1 - 2 t pepper, freshly ground 1 T dill weed, fresh, minced 2 T olive oil 1 medium onion, peel and thinly sliced 1 red and yellow bell pepper, remove core and seeds, finely chop 1 c celery, trim and finely chop 2 cloves garlic, peeled and minced 2 T (about) margarine or butter 1 lemon	Preheat oven to 400. Sprinkle pepper and dill weed on both sides of fish steaks and set aside. Heat olive oil in nonstick pan on medium-high heat. Add celery, onion, and peppers to pan and sauté until begins to soften (about 5 minutes). Add garlic and sauté until fragrant (about 1 minute) and take off heat. Put each steak in foil (large enough piece to seal it with veggies on top and small amount of air space). Put veggie mixture in steak cavity and on top of steak. Dot margarine or butter on top of veggies. Squeeze fresh lemon juice over veggies. Close foil leaving small air space on top (for steam circulation). Bake for 25 to 30 minutes or until fish flakes with fork.

Wendy Hull, a Soldiers' Angel in Cottage Grove, Oregon

Smoked Salmon Spread with Baguette

6 oz smoked salmon, chopped 16 oz cream cheese, softened 1 sourdough baguette, sliced thinly into 32 slices fresh dill, for garnish 1 tomato, chopped, for garnish capers, for garnish	Combine the salmon and the cream cheese until thoroughly blended. Serve with baguette and garnishes.

Vanessa Bishop, a Soldiers' Angel in Texas

Pennsylvania

Bonnie's Orange Jell-O Salad

1 (6-oz) box orange Jell-O 2 c boiling water 1 (6-oz) can frozen orange juice (NOT thawed) 1 large can Mandarin oranges, drained (reserve a few for garnish if desired) 1⅔ c crushed pineapple, NOT drained (a bit less than a full large can, do not use all of the can as the Jell-O will be too soft)	This is great for picnics or when the food will be set out for a while, it holds its shape without melting, it's also wonderful if there are leftovers. In a large bowl, mix Jell-O and boiling water until well dissolved. Add frozen orange juice and stir until dissolved. Cool for about 15 minutes. Add pineapple and oranges, stir gently. Pour into a mold if desired. Refrigerate to set. I usually make this the night before or early in the morning before it's needed. It probably needs a minimum of 4 hours in the refrigerator. When ready to serve, unmold onto a plate. You may garnish with dollops of whipped cream and place the reserved oranges on top.

Anita Betschart, a Soldiers' Angel in McDonald, Pennsylvania

Broccoli Cheese Soup with Noodles

2 - 3 small onions 6 c chicken broth 12 oz egg noodles 10 oz frozen chopped broccoli 3¼ c milk ½ lb white American cheese 1 lb Velveeta cheese ¼ c butter	Sauté onions in butter in a large pot. Add chicken broth and bring to a boil. Add egg noodles and boil 4 minutes, keep stirring. Add broccoli and boil another 4 minutes. Add milk. Add both cheeses gradually while stirring until completely melted. Enjoy!

Michele McGovern, a Soldiers' Angel in Lebanon, Pennsylvania

Buffalo Chicken Dip

2 (8-oz) cans chicken 1 c Ranch dressing ½ c red hot sauce 2 (8-oz) pkg cream cheese 1 pkg shredded mild Cheddar cheese 1 bag tortilla chips, for serving	Mix all ingredients except Cheddar cheese and chips, and bake in 9 x 9 baking dish at 350 for 30 to 40 minutes or until bubbling. Top with cheese. You can substitute the ranch with ½ cup crumbled blue cheese and ½ cup blue cheese dressing.

Laura Stedila, a Soldiers' Angel in Pittsburgh, Pennsylvania

Chicken with Lemony Egg Noodles and Peas

8 oz extra wide noodles 4 oz sugar snap peas 1 c shredded carrots 1 c frozen peas 1 c chicken broth ½ c heavy or whipping cream 1 t fresh lemon peel ½ t ground pepper ½ t salt 2 c (10 oz) skinless chicken meat	Heat 4-quart covered saucepan of salted water to boiling over high heat. Add noodles and cook as label directs, but add snap peas to noodles 1 minute before noodles are done. Place carrots and frozen peas in colander in sink. Drain noodles and snap peas over carrots and frozen peas. While noodle mixture drains, in same saucepan, heat broth, cream, lemon peel, pepper, and salt to boiling. Stir chicken and noodle mixture into sauce: heat through, stirring constantly.

RaeAnn Gordon, a Soldiers' Angel in Coraopolis, Pennsylvania

Cherry Chocolate Cake

1 pkg chocolate cake mix 3 eggs 1 can cherry fruit filling 1 c sugar 5 T butter ⅓ c milk 1 (6-oz) pkg semisweet chocolate pieces	Combine cake mix, eggs, and cherry fruit filling. Mix until well blended. Pour into greased and floured 9 x 13 inch pan. Bake at 350 for 35 to 40 minutes. Frost when cool with following: In a small saucepan combine sugar, butter and milk. Bring to boil, stirring constantly and cook 1 minute. Remove from heat, stir in chocolate pieces until melted and smooth. Spread over cake.

Leigh, a Soldiers' Angel in Strasburg, Pennsylvania

Crock Pot Chicken

6 boneless, skinless chicken breasts 6 slices Swiss cheese (or can substitute 1½ c shredded Cheddar cheese) 1 can cream of mushroom soup ¼ c milk 2 c herb seasoned stuffing mix ½ c butter, melted	This recipe reminds us of Thanksgiving dinner. Spray crock pot with non-stick cooking oil. Arrange chicken in the crock pot. Top the chicken with the cheese. Combine the cream of mushroom soup and milk, mix well. Spoon the soup mix evenly over the cheese. Sprinkle with stuffing mix. Drizzle the melted butter over the stuffing. Cook in the crock pot on low for 8 hours. Enjoy!

Michele McGovern, a Soldiers' Angel in Lebanon, Pennsylvania

Deer Steaks

2 – 4 deer steaks 1 pouch onion soup mix 2 cans GOLDEN mushroom soup 1 soup can water extra (real) onion sliced (if desired)	Spray 9 x 13 baking dish with cooking spray. Lay steaks in pan (if desired, slice real onions on top of steak). In separate bowl, whisk soup mix, mushroom soup, and water. Pour contents over steaks. Cover with foil and bake at 350 for at least 1½ to 2 hours (depending upon thickness of steak). Check after an hour to be sure steaks don't dry out. Golden mushroom soup will thicken into "gravy". The extra onions will take out the "game taste". Can be used for chops also.

Pam Hawk, a Soldiers' Angel Freeport, Pennsylvania

Easy One-pan Chocolate Cake

⅓ c vegetable oil 2 oz unsweetened chocolate ¾ c water 1 c sugar 1 egg 1¼ c all purpose flour ½ t salt ½ t baking soda 1 t vanilla 6 oz chocolate chips (I like to use the mini chips) ⅓ c chopped nuts (optional) whipped cream, Cool Whip, or vanilla ice cream, for serving	Preheat oven to 350. While the oven is heating, put chocolate and oil into an 8-inch square baking pan and place that in the oven for the chocolate to melt, about 4 minutes. When melted, remove from oven and stir gently with a fork to mix; let cool a few minutes. Add the sugar and stir well. If you want, combine the flour, salt and baking soda (this is optional). Add all other ingredients except the chips and nuts. There is no set order, but I usually add part of the water, then egg, part of the flour/salt/soda and repeat the water and flour till it's all mixed, adding the vanilla last. Beat with a fork (or a small whisk if you have one) until smooth, about 1 minute. Scrape sides of pan with a spatula. Sprinkle chips and nuts evenly on top. (Or you can mix half into the batter and half on top). Bake for 40 minutes or until a toothpick comes out clean. Cool. Serve with topping or plain. This is a very moist cake and will disappear very quickly. If you make a pan for yourself and have leftovers, it stays moist for quite a while. It will also freeze well.

Anita Betschart, a Soldiers' Angel in McDonald, Pennsylvania

Ham Sandwich

1 lb chipped ham (has too be chipped or cut in small pieces with a knife) ½ lb cubed American cheese 3 hard boiled eggs (cut up in small pieces) 1 c mayonnaise ½ c ketchup	Mix together and put on hamburger rolls. Wrap them in foil, individually. You can freeze them for later. Heat oven to 400. Bake about 20 minutes if fresh and 35 to 45 minutes if frozen. The time frozen depends on your oven.

Sandra Myers, a Soldiers' Angel in Pennsylvania

Hash Brown Casserole

1 (32-oz) pkg frozen cubed hash brown potatoes, thawed ¾ c butter, divided (melt ¼ c) ½ c chopped onion (1 small onion) 8 oz sour cream 1½ c shredded Cheddar cheese 2 c corn flakes 1 (10¾-oz) can cream of chicken soup	Preheat oven to 350. Combine the thawed hash browns, 1/2 cup unmelted butter, onions, sour cream, cheese, and cream of chicken soup. Mix well and put in a greased 9 x 13 inch casserole dish. Crush the corn flakes and add the 1/4 cup melted butter to them and mix well. Sprinkle the corn flake mixture evenly on top of the potato mixture. Bake for 50 to 60 minutes. Enjoy! Note: Can also add cooked chopped chicken to the dish. Or you can convert the recipe to a breakfast casserole by eliminating the cream of chicken soup and cooked chicken and adding 12 eggs (scrambled with a fork) to the potato mixture instead.

Michele McGovern, a Soldiers' Angel in Lebanon, Pennsylvania

Hot Roast Beef Sandwiches

1 rump roast (4 - 5 lb) 1 jar pepperoncini peppers (look in your supermarket where the Italian foods and condiments are; if I have a slightly smaller roast, I use a small jar, and if I use a larger roast I go for a large jar) 1 lb good sharp Provolone cheese, preferably Asiago, if available sub rolls/hoagie rolls, for serving	Place the roast in the crock pot and pour the pepperoncini peppers with all of the liquid that is in the jar, into the crock pot. Place the lid on and cook according to your crock pot directions. Pull the meat apart when done, (it tends to fall apart anyhow when it's cooked). Keep warm in all the wonderful juices from the meat and the peppers. Serve on a roll with some Asiago cheese. Add a little salt and pepper. That's it! Good meat, good cheese, pepperoncini peppers and the most important ingredient.... good bread make this a no brainer. Mmmm Mmmm Mmmm! It doesn't get any easier and people won't believe that's all there was to it. In fact, don't tell them. Sshhhh, it can be a secret recipe.

Kathy, a Soldiers' Angel in Upper Darby, Pennsylvania

Mom's Bar-B-Que Sauce

1 T butter, margarine, or oil 1 medium onion, diced 1 stalk celery, diced (small pieces) 1 can tomato sauce (can use no-salt if you like) ½ c ketchup ⅓ c water 1 T brown sugar 1 T prepared mustard lemon juice or vinegar to taste (1 - 2 t) 1 lb chipped ham (this was a specialty of Isalys Deli in Pittsburgh, PA; use boiled or baked ham, have the deli slice it as thin as they can, thus the term "chipped"; add whole slices or cut the pile of meat into strips, no need to be precise, you just want the meet to fit on the bun) buns, for serving	This is not a "traditional" bbq sauce but one my mom has made for sandwiches since I was a little kid. Sauté onions and celery in butter until soft. Add remaining sauce ingredients and simmer about 15 minutes. Add meat and heat through. Serve on sandwich buns. This is good as a quick meal with carrot and celery sticks, chips, etc, and is also quite good as leftovers.

Anita Betschart, a Soldiers' Angel in McDonald, Pennsylvania

Mom's Best Ever Meatloaf

1½ lb lean ground beef 1 c seasoned bread crumbs ½ c chopped onion (1 small onion) 1 egg 1 t salt ⅛ t pepper 1 can Manwich 2 T yellow mustard, divided	Preheat oven to 350. Combine the ground beef, bread crumbs, onion, egg, salt, pepper, and 1 tablespoon of yellow mustard with 1/2 cup of the Manwich, mix well. Shape into a loaf and place in baking dish. Bake for 45 minutes. Drain fat. Add remaining 1 tablespoon yellow mustard to the remaining Manwich and pour mixture on meatloaf, spreading evenly. Bake 35 minutes longer, basting if necessary. Enjoy!

Michele McGovern, a Soldiers' Angel in Lebanon, Pennsylvania

Pittsburgh Stuffing

1 c onion, chopped 1 c celery, sliced ¼ c butter or margarine 1 c tart apple, cored and chopped 1 c chopped walnuts or pecans 1 c raisins 1 pkg (8- to 10-oz) herb-flavored stuffing mix, prepared	In a saucepan, sauté onion and celery in butter or margarine. Stir in apple, nuts, and raisins. Toss mixture with prepared stuffing. Spoon into greased 1½ quart baking dish. For a moist stuffing, cover during baking. For a drier stuffing, bake uncovered. Bake at 350 for 30 minutes or until heated through.

Doreas_13, a Soldiers' Angel in Pennsylvania

Pull-apart Bread

1 (10-roll) tube refrigerated biscuits 1 (16-oz) jar salsa 1 (8-oz) pkg shredded cheese	Open tube of biscuits and cut each one into quarters to make 40 biscuits. Put into a bowl. Pour salsa over the biscuits. Add ¾ of the cheese. Stir gently to cover all biscuits with salsa and cheese. Spray a 13 x 9 inch pan with cooking spray. Spread biscuits in pan. Bake at 375 for 35 minutes. Sprinkle remaining cheese on top. Bake 10 more minutes. Excellent hot or cold, and can be reheated in the microwave. Optional toppings include onions, black olives, green peppers, or jalapeño peppers.

Pam Hawk, a Soldiers' Angel in Freeport, Pennsylvania

Pumpkin Gingerbread Trifle

2 (14-oz) boxes gingerbread mix 1 (5.1-oz) box cook-and-serve vanilla pudding mix 1 (30-oz) can pumpkin pie filling ½ c packed brown sugar ⅓ t ground cardamom or cinnamon 1 (12-oz) container frozen whipped topping, thawed ½ c gingersnap cookies (optional)	Bake the gingerbread according to package directions, cool completely. Meanwhile, prepare the pudding and set aside to cool. Stir the pumpkin pie filling, brown sugar, and cardamom or cinnamon into the cooled pudding. Crumble 1 batch of the gingerbread into the bottom of a large pretty bowl. Pour 1/2 of the pudding mixture over the crumbled gingerbread. Add a layer of whipped topping. Repeat with the remaining gingerbread, pudding and whipped topping. Sprinkle the top with crushed gingersnaps if desired. Refrigerate overnight. Enjoy!

Michele McGovern, a Soldiers' Angel in Lebanon, Pennsylvania

Pumpkin Whoopie Pies

2 c brown sugar 1 c vegetable oil ½ c cooked, mashed pumpkin 2 eggs 3 c flour 1 t salt 1 t baking powder 1 t baking soda 1 t vanilla ½ T cinnamon ½ T ginger ½ T ground cloves 1 egg white, beaten 2 T milk 1 t vanilla 2 c powdered sugar ¾ c shortening	Cream sugar and oil. Add pumpkin and eggs. Add flour, salt, baking powder, baking soda, 1 teaspoon vanilla, and spices; mix well. Drop by heaping teaspoons onto greased cookie sheet. Bake at 350 for 10 to 12 minutes. For filling, mix egg white, milk, remaining teaspoon vanilla, and 1 cup powdered sugar. Then add second cup of powdered sugar and the shortening. Spread dab of filling on flat side of cookie. Top with another cookie to form a sandwich.

Leigh, a Soldiers' Angel in Strasburg, Pennsylvania

Sloppy Joes

1 lb hamburger ½ c ketchup 1 T vinegar 1 T Worcestershire sauce touch of salt and pepper 1 small onion, chopped 1 small green pepper, chopped hamburger buns, for serving	Cook the hamburger and drain off the grease. Add everything in a pot and simmer for however long you want, stirring often so as not to burn it. Don't put in a crock pot, it gets too runny. Use the cheap hamburger, because for some reason it tastes better with cheap. Plus, it always tastes better the next day. Put on hamburger buns and serve.

Sandi Myers, a Soldiers' Angel in Pennsylvania

Stuffed Shells

1½ lb hamburger (can be all beef or turkey or a mix of beef and turkey) 1 chopped onion (amount your preference) chopped garlic (amount your preference) 2 boxes chopped spinach, thawed and squeezed dry 2 eggs 1 (8-oz) pkg cream cheese, softened ⅔ c Parmesan cheese 1 large bottle Ragu Sauce 1 box jumbo shells, cooked (about 25 - 30) mozzarella cheese (optional)	Brown hamburger with onion and garlic; add salt and pepper to taste, if desired. Mix burger mixture with cream cheese, eggs, Parmesan cheese, and spinach. Spray 13 x 9 x 2 casserole pan with cooking spray; put a small amount of sauce on bottom of pan. Stuff shells with mixture. Add stuffed shells to pan. Cover with remaining sauce. Cover with mozzarella cheese, if desired. Bake at 350 for 45 to 60 minutes. Can be made ahead of time and frozen. Freezes well.

Pam Hawk, a Soldiers' Angel in Freeport, Pennsylvania

Whoopie Pies

2 c sugar 1 c shortening 1 c cocoa 2 egg yolks and 2 whole eggs 2 t vanilla 1 c sour milk or buttermilk 2 t baking soda ½ t salt 4 c flour 2 egg whites 1 box confectioner sugar 1 c shortening 4 T milk 1 t vanilla	Cream sugar and shortening together in a large bowl. Add eggs and mix. Sift dry ingredients together and add to the creamed mixture alternatively with milk. Batter will be stiff. If it is too thin, add more flour. Drop by tablespoon onto greased sheets. Bake at 350 for 8 to 10 minutes, until a toothpick inserted in the cookies comes out clean. For the filling, beat egg whites until stiff. Add shortening and vanilla and blend. Add milk and then add the sugar. Beat until smooth. Spread some filling on the bottom side of one cookie; top with a second cookie. Repeat with the remaining cookies and filling. Store in the refrigerator or freezer.

Anne Hartley, a Soldiers' Angel in Texas

Rhode Island

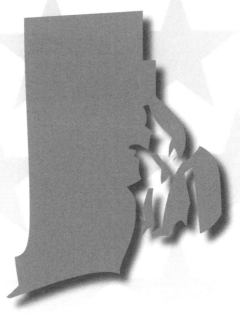

Clam Cakes

2 ½ c flour 1 t sugar ½ t salt 4 t baking powder 3 eggs ½ c milk 1 c clam broth 2 c chopped clams (preferably quahogs) vegetable oil (enough for deep frying)	In a large bowl, mix all the ingredients (except the oil) until smooth. In a deep fryer or heavy saucepan, heat the oil to 350. Carefully add small scoops of batter (approximately 1 tablespoon each) to the hot oil and cook until each clam cake is golden brown on all sides. Drain on paper towels. Serve hot. Makes 24 servings. (Clam cakes are best served alongside a big bowl of steaming clam chowder!)

Nicolle Belesimo, a Soldiers' Angel in Johnston, Rhode Island

Clam Chowder

16 c (1 gal) clam juice ¼ lb salt pork, chopped ½ c diced onions 8 lb all-purpose potatoes, peeled and diced in ½-inch pieces 1 T white pepper 1 T Worcestershire sauce 2 c chopped, cooked clams (preferably quahogs)	In a large stockpot, heat the clam juice just to a simmer, then cover and set aside. In a frying pan, fry the salt pork. When the fat is cooked out, remove the salt pork and set aside. Sauté the onions in the fat until they are tender and translucent. Do not allow the onions to turn brown. Put the stockpot back on the heat. Add the onions to the clam juice and bring to a simmer. Add the potatoes and simmer until tender. Add the fried salt pork, pepper and Worcestershire sauce. Add the chopped clams. Heat thoroughly and serve. Makes 20 servings.

Nicolle Belesimo, a Soldiers' Angel in Johnston, Rhode Island

Coffee Cabinet

1 c very strong coffee 1 c sugar ½ t vanilla 1 scoop vanilla ice cream 6 oz milk	In a small saucepan, heat coffee to just simmering. Stir in sugar and vanilla and simmer 8 minutes, stirring constantly to ensure that all of the sugar is dissolved. Remove from heat and cool completely. Add the ice cream, milk and 2 tablespoons of the cooled coffee syrup* to a blender and blend until smooth. Pour into a glass and serve immediately. Makes 1 serving. *Leftover coffee syrup can be stored in the refrigerator for up to 2 weeks and is great served over ice cream or mixed into a glass of milk.

Nicolle Belesimo, a Soldiers' Angel in Johnston, Rhode Island

Frozen Lemonade

1½ c sugar 1 c water 1 envelope plain gelatin 2 T cold water 2 egg whites 2 T sugar 1½ c fresh lemon juice 1 T finely chopped lemon rind	In a saucepan, boil the 1½ cups sugar and 1 cup water to make a simple syrup solution. Remove from heat. Soften the gelatin in the 2 tablespoons of cold water and add to the saucepan with the simple syrup. Stir until dissolved and set aside to cool. Beat the egg whites until light, adding the 2 tablespoons sugar. Continue beating until stiff peaks form. Combine the beaten egg whites with the simple syrup mixture. Add the lemon juice and rind and stir until blended. Pour the mixture into an ice cube tray and freeze until set. Once frozen, put the frozen cubes into a blender. Process the cubes until they have a slushy consistency. Pour into serving glasses and enjoy!

Nicolle Belesimo, a Soldiers' Angel in Johnston, Rhode Island

Johnnycakes

2 c stone-ground cornmeal ½ t salt ¾ c cold water 1½ c milk 1 t sugar (optional)	Combine the cornmeal, salt, water and sugar. Add the milk and stir until smooth. Heat a well-oiled frying pan over medium heat until hot. Carefully ladle the batter into the hot pan to make cakes approximately 3 inches in size. Fry for 2 minutes, or until the edges of the johnnycakes turn brown. Flip each johnnycake over to cook for 1 minute on the other side. Remove from the pan and serve immediately with butter and maple syrup. Makes 6 to 8 servings.

Nicolle Belesimo, a Soldiers' Angel in Johnston, Rhode Island

Red Clam Chowder

¼ c bacon, finely cut up ¼ c onion, finely chopped 2 (8-oz) cans minced or whole clams 2 c potatoes, peeled and finely chopped 1 c water ⅓ c celery, chopped 1 (16-oz) can whole tomatoes, undrained 2 t fresh parsley, chopped 1 t salt ¼ t dried thyme ⅛ t pepper oyster crackers, for serving (optional)	Cook and stir bacon and onion in large kettle until bacon is crisp and onion is tender. Drain clams, reserving liquid. Add clam liquid, potatoes, water, and celery to bacon and onion. Cook until potatoes are tender, about 10 minutes. Add clams, tomatoes, parsley, salt, thyme and pepper. Heat to boiling, stirring occasionally. Serve with oyster crackers, if desired.

Donna Allon (fefifauxfumgirl), a Soldiers' Angel in Alabama

Presbyterian Bars

6 c Special K cereal 1 c sugar 1 c white Karo syrup ½ c butter 2½ c crunchy peanut butter 1 (6-oz) pkg chocolate chips 1 (6-oz) pkg butterscotch chips	Bring to boil sugar, syrup. and butter. Add peanut butter. Pour over cereal. Mix and press into 13 x 9 cake pan. Melt chocolate chips and butterscotch chips together. Frost bars. Chill before cutting.

Paula M Tucci, CTL for Providence VA Medical Center and a Soldiers' Angel in Cumberland, Rhode Island

Venus de Milo Soup

1 medium onion, chopped 2 T butter ¾ - 1 lb extra lean ground hamburger, crumbled and browned salt and pepper to taste 1 (14.5-oz) can stewed tomatoes put through the blender 4 tomato cans water 4 beef bouillon cubes 1 (10-oz) pkg mixed vegetables (or 1 or 2 cans VegAll) ½ c small shell pasta	Sauté onion in 1 tablespoon butter. Add hamburger and salt and pepper to taste. Add stewed tomatoes, water, bouillon cubes, and vegetables. Cook for 15 to 20 minutes. Add pasta. Cook 10 to 15 minutes longer. This recipe was devised by Emeril Lagasse for Swansea in Massachusetts when he worked there while attending Johnson & Wales University in Rhode Island.

Paula M Tucci, CTL for Providence VA Medical Center and a Soldiers' Angel in Cumberland, Rhode Island

South Carolina

Chocolate Zucchini Bread

3 eggs 1 c oil 2 t vanilla 2 c sugar 3 c grated zucchini 2⅓ c flour ½ c cocoa 2 t soda 1 t cinnamon 1 t salt ¼ t baking powder ½ c each nuts and chocolate chips	Mix all ingredients and bake at 350 for 45 minutes in 2 greased 9 x 5 inch loaf pans.

Lara Pennell, a Soldiers' Angel in Mauldin, South Carolina

Cinnamon "Pinch" Rolls

2 loaves of frozen bread, thawed 2 sticks butter or margarine 1 c brown sugar 1 small box vanilla pudding (NOT instant) 2 – 3 T milk ground cinnamon, as desired nuts (optional)	Spray 9 x 13 glass baking dish with cooking spray. Pinch off pieces of bread dough and fill dish. Melt butter or margarine; add sugar, pudding, milk, cinnamon (and nuts if desired). Stir well. Pour over bread pieces. Spray wax paper with cooking spray and cover dish. Let rise overnight. Bake next morning at 350 for approximately 30 minutes (check at 25 minutes). Serve warm.

Cody Hawk, United States Navy, Goose Creek, South Carolina

Cranberry Pumpkin Bread

2 eggs 2 c sugar ½ c oil 1 c pumpkin 2¼ c flour 1 T pumpkin pie spice 1 t soda ½ t salt 1 c fresh or frozen cranberries, sliced	Mix all ingredients just until incorporated but not until smooth. Put into 2 greased floured bread pans. Bake at 350 for 1 hour.

Lara Pennell, a Soldiers' Angel in Mauldin, South Carolina

Lara's Buttermilk Scones with Devonshire Cream and Lemon Curd

2 c flour ⅓ c plus ¾ c sugar 1½ t baking powder ½ t baking soda ¼ t salt 6 T plus ¼ c butter ⅔ c buttermilk 5 eggs 1½ t vanilla (I use less) ½ c whipping cream, whipped 1½ c sour cream 2 T powdered sugar rind of 1 lemon ½ c fresh lemon juice	Mix flour, sugar, baking powder, baking soda, and salt. Cut in 6 tablespoons butter. Mix 2 eggs, vanilla, and buttermilk. Fold in. Cut into scones. (May be frozen at this point. Put in single layer on cookie sheet. When frozen put in zippered plastic bag. Increase baking time 5 to 7 minutes.) Bake at 350 for 25 minutes. Mix whipping cream, sour cream, and powdered sugar to make Mock Devonshire Cream. Serve with scones. For Lemon Curd, mix 3 eggs, rind of 1 lemon, lemon juice, ¾ c sugar, and ¼ c butter cut into small pieces. Cook over double boiler for 10 minutes or until it coats spoon OR cook over direct heat and stir constantly. "Zap" it with blender stick to make it smooth. Refrigerate. Serve with scones.

Lara Pennell, a Soldiers' Angel in Mauldin, South Carolina

Mean Beans

1 (16-oz) can refried beans (your favorite brand and flavor) 1 lb ground beef or turkey or mix onion, garlic, red or green peppers chilies or olives, as desired 1 (16-oz) jar salsa – your favorite brand and degree of hot 2 c grated Taco cheese or Mexican (Cheddar is also good) tortilla chips, for serving	Spray 9 x 9 inch baking dish with cooking spray. Spread refried beans onto bottom of baking dish. In separate pan, brown meat, onion, garlic, pepper, and others per your taste. (Ready when meat is cooked and onions are tender.) Spread over beans in baking dish. Cover meat mixture with salsa. Cover salsa with cheese. (All of the above can be done ahead of time – "before the party". Store in fridge until ready to bake. Bake a half hour before you are ready to serve.) Bake approximately 30 minutes until hot the whole way through. Serve warm with your favorite tortilla chips. This is called "Mean Beans" because you can make this as HOT as you want! For 9 x 13 baking dish, double the ingredients.

Cody Hawk, United States Navy, Goose Creek, South Carolina

Michael's Favorite Pancakes

1 c flour 1½ c buttermilk 1 t salt 1 t baking powder 1 ½ t sugar ½ t baking soda 1 egg Extras: baking chips, banana slices, apple slices, pumpkin, spices, etc	Stir all ingredients just until incorporated, will be slightly lumpy. Cook on hot griddle.

Lara Pennell, a Soldiers' Angel in Mauldin, South Carolina

Rhubarb Coffee Cake	
1½ c plus ½ c sugar ½ c plus 1 T butter 1 egg 1 T vanilla 1 c buttermilk 1 t soda 2 c plus 1 T flour 1½ c fresh or frozen rhubarb	Beat 1½ cups sugar, ½ c butter, egg, vanilla, buttermilk, soda, and 2 cups flour. Stir in rhubarb. Pour into greased 9 x 13 inch pan. Cut ½ cup sugar, 1 teaspoon flour, cinnamon, and 1 tablespoon butter to make topping. Sprinkle rhubarb with topping. Bake at 350 for 35 to 40 minutes.

Lara Pennell, a Soldiers' Angel in Mauldin, South Carolina

South Carolina Low-Country Boil (Frogmore Stew)	
4 qt water 1 pkg crab/shrimp boil 3 T kosher salt 1 can beer (optional) 1 lemon, cut in half 1 medium onion 12 new potatoes 2 lb spicy sausage (chorizo or Italian sausage) 6 ears corn cut in half (fresh is best, but frozen is ok) 2 lb raw shrimp, leave the peel on butter, for serving	Bring water, boil, and salt to a boil in a covered 8-quart pot (may need an even larger pot). Once boiling, add beer, lemon, onion, potatoes, and corn. Cover and boil 10 minutes; add the sausage and boil another 6 minutes, and then add the shrimp and cook for another 6 minutes. Melt a stick of butter for the shrimp, potatoes, and corn. This would make enough for 4 people. I usually allow ½ lb shrimp and ½ lb of sausage per person, so this makes it easy to increase if needed.

Sandi Mills, a Soldiers' Angel in Greenville, South Carolina

South Dakota

Rice and Hamburger Hot Dish

¾ c uncooked white Minute Rice 1 c diced celery 1 medium onion, chopped 1 can cream of chicken soup 1 can water 1 lb hamburger 1 t salt 1 T soy sauce	Stir soup and water to get rid of lumps. Brown hamburger and sauté celery and onion. Drain off grease. Combine all ingredients in casserole. Cook uncovered, 1 hour at 350. Stir often. Add a little extra water if it starts to dry out.

Linda, a Soldiers' Angel in California

The State Dessert of South Dakota

1 pkg dry yeast 1 T sugar ¼ c lukewarm water 2 c warm milk 2 eggs ½ c shortening 6 - 8 c flour ½ c sugar 1 t salt 2 c sweet cream or sour cream 2 eggs, beaten ½ c sugar 2 T flour ½ t vanilla fruit cinnamon	Dissolve yeast and 1 tablespoon sugar in lukewarm water. Combine milk and 2 eggs; beat well. Add shortening, beat again. In a large bowl, combine flour, ½ cup sugar, and salt and add first mixture to it. Mix well. Knead until dough is smooth and elastic, sprinkle with a little flour at a time. Put in warm place to rise until double in bulk. Divide dough into 8 equal parts. Roll each piece to fit a pie plate. Let rise 20 minutes. Put fruit on top (can use apples, peaches, raisins, or prunes). Top the fruit with cream filling. Sprinkle with cinnamon. Bake at 350 for 25 to 30 minutes or until brown.

Linda McWeeney, a Soldiers' Angel in California

Tennessee

Cherry Pie Brownies

1 box dark chocolate brownie mix 1 can cherry pie filling	Preheat oven to 350 and line 9 x 13-inch pan with nonstick aluminum foil, overlapping ends (easier to lift out of pan this way). Follow the recipe on the box but substitute the cherry pie filling for one egg. Bake until center springs back. Cool completely, lift foil and brownies out of pan and cut into squares.

Patsy Ruppe, a Soldiers' Angel in Kingston, Tennessee

Chocolate Coconut Cookie Bars

1 box chocolate cake mix 1 stick softened butter or margarine 1 egg 1 bag coconut 1 can sweetened condensed milk 2 bags chocolate chips	Preheat oven to 350; line 9 x 13-inch pan with nonstick aluminum foil, overlapping ends (easier to lift out of pan this way). Mix cake mix, butter, and egg until crumbly and starts to stick together, spread onto bottom of pan. Bake 15 to 20 minutes until lightly browned (starts to set). Remove from oven. Sprinkle coconut over baked mixture and pour sweetened condensed milk over coconut. Return to oven and bake 15 to 20 minutes or until coconut browns. In double boiler, melt 2 bags chocolate chips. Pour evenly over coconut, cool completely (may have to put into the refrigerator at the last part of the cooling to completely set the chocolate). Lift foil out of pan and cut into squares.

Patsy Ruppe, a Soldiers' Angel in Kingston, Tennessee

Hoppin' John

1 c small dried peas such as cowpeas or black-eyes 5 - 6 c water 1 dried hot pepper (optional) 1 smoked ham hock 1 medium onion, chopped (about ¾ c) 1 c long-grain white rice	Wash and sort the peas. Place them in a saucepan, add the water and discard any peas that float. Gently boil the peas with the pepper, ham hock, and onion, uncovered, until tender but not mushy, about 1½ hours or until 2 cups of liquid remain. Add the rice to the pot, cover and simmer over low heat for about 20 minutes, never lifting the lid. Remove from the heat and allow to steam, still covered, for another 10 minutes. Remove the cover, fluff with a fork and serve.

Iris Wilde, a Soldiers' Angel in Wisconsin

Pecan Pie Cookie Bars

1 box yellow cake mix (reserve 2/3 cup) 1 stick butter or margarine (softened not melted) 4 eggs 1½ c Karo syrup ½ c brown sugar 1 t vanilla 1 c chopped pecans	Preheat oven to 350 and line 9 x 13-inch pan with nonstick aluminum foil, overlapping ends (easier to lift out of pan this way). Blend cake mix, butter, and 1 egg; press into bottom of pan, bake for 15 to 20 minutes until golden brown. While crust is baking, mix syrup, brown sugar, vanilla, 3 eggs, reserved cake mix, and chopped pecans. Pour over baked crust and return to oven for 30 to 35 minutes until center is set. Cool completely, lift foil out of pan, and cut into squares. (I found an extra large pizza cutter that works great for cutting these sticky goodies, just dip in warm water before you start cutting and it just slices right through.)

Patsy Ruppe, a Soldiers' Angel in Kingston, Tennessee

Sweet Tea (Sun Tea)	
4 -5 ice tea bags sugar to taste	Fill a big glass jar container (about 2 gallon size) with water and add tea bags. Experiment and you will find how many you like....start with 4 or 5 small tea bags). Place ice tea bags in container and set outside in the sun. When it is strong enough to your liking, bring in and put sugar in tea. No Southern home would be without their sweet tea! If you ever visit a Southern state, you MUST specify that you want unsweetened tea or it will be served sweet in almost all restaurants.

Iris Wilde, a Soldiers' Angel in Wisconsin

Texas

Banana Split Salad

1 large carton frozen whipped topping, thawed 1 can evaporated milk 1 can cherry pie filling 1 (8-oz) can crushed pineapple, drained 4 chopped bananas ½ c chopped pecans	Beat whipped topping and milk. Fold in other ingredients. Chill until serving time.

Dean Datel, a Soldiers' Angel in Texas

Better Than Sex Cake

1 large can crushed pineapple 1 c sugar 1 box yellow cake mix 1 large box instant vanilla pudding 3 - 4 bananas 1 large container frozen whipped topping, thawed 1 c chopped nuts 1 c shredded coconut	Bake cake as directed. Bake in a 9 x 12 inch pan. Mix pineapple and sugar in a pot, and cook on medium heat until thickened; set aside, Make pudding as directed and set aside. When cake has cooled, pierce all over with a fork. Spread the pineapple mixture over the cake. Top with sliced bananas, pudding, whipped topping, chopped nuts and coconut. Chill. This cake must be refrigerated.

Dean Datel, a Soldiers' Angel in Texas

Breakfast Casserole

12 slices bacon 3 c croutons (preferably home made) 2 c grated Cheddar or Swiss cheese 6 eggs 2 T olive oil 1½ c half-and-half 1 white onion, thinly sliced 1 green bell pepper, thinly sliced 1 red bell pepper, thinly sliced 1 T Dijon mustard salt and pepper to taste	Cook bacon until crispy. Drain, crumble, and set aside. Sauté onion until golden in olive oil, about 20 minutes. Preheat oven to 325. Rub olive oil in the bottom of a 9 x 12-inch baking dish. Place croutons in the bottom of the dish and sprinkle with grated cheese. Crack the eggs into a bowl, whisking to break up the yolks. Add half-and-half, sautéed onions, peppers, mustard, salt, and pepper, and beat until well combined. Pour over the croutons and cheese, and sprinkle with crumbled bacon. Bake in the preheated oven for 40 minutes. Remove from oven and allow to stand 10 minutes before serving. Top with chives.

Texas 0302, a Soldiers' Angel in Texas

Chili

1 pkg stew meat, cut into bite-size pieces 1 pkg Italian sausage, ground 1 lb ground beef 6 (8-oz) cans tomato sauce 1 can Mexican diced tomatoes 3 cans kidney beans, drained 2 cans black beans, drained 3 T chili powder 1 t paprika 1 t red pepper 1 t ground jalapeño 1 t garlic powder 3 t dried onion 1 jalapeño, diced	Dump all cans into a pot with the spices. Fry meats, one at a time, and add to sauce. Let cook for about 3 hours on low heat. Stir often to keep from sticking. Serve with rice, crackers, and corn chips; top with onions, cheese, lettuce, and tomatoes.

Kim Hightower, Houston VACTL, a Soldiers' Angel in La Porte, Texas

Dean's Famous Chocolate Chip Cake

1 box yellow cake mix 2 pkg (small) chocolate instant pudding 4 eggs 12 oz chocolate chips ½ c oil 1½ c water 1 t vanilla	Mill all ingredients. Coat chocolate chips in flour so chips do not sink (I use a colander for this.) Bake at 350 degrees in Bundt pan. Easy and good.

Dean Datel, a Soldiers' Angel in Texas

Easy Cheesy Quiso

3 lb Velveeta 1 can Rotel tomatoes 1 lb ground beef 1 can chicken enchilada soup 1 large bag nacho chips	In a 3-quart crock pot, cut cheese into cubes to speed melting. Brown ground beef in skillet, crumble, and add to crock pot. Add tomatoes and soup, stir well. Heat on high until cheese is melted, stirring often. Reduce heat and serve with chips. The soup makes a nice addition to the dish.

Carla Gamblin, a Soldiers' Angel in Tyler, Texas

Easy Peach Cobbler

1 stick butter 1 c self-rising flour 1 c sugar 1 c milk large can sliced peaches with heavy syrup dash vanilla dash cinnamon	Melt butter in a casserole dish. Mix flour, sugar, and milk. Can add a dash of vanilla and a dash of cinnamon. Pour peaches and syrup and batter into the casserole dish. Put in 350 oven and cook until top turns golden brown. Delicious and very short prep time.

Dean Datel, a Soldiers' Angel in Texas

Fresh Tomato Salsa

1½ lb ripe tomatoes, seeded, chopped 1 medium purple onion, chopped 1 large clove garlic, chopped 3 scallions or green onions, chopped 1 - 2 large fresh jalapeño pepper, seeded, chopped ¼ c fresh cilantro leaves, chopped 1 - 3 small cans of green chilies, depending upon taste 1 T olive oil 2 T fresh lime juice ½ t salt ¼ t ground cumin 1 t red wine vinegar 2 T tomato juice	Combine onion, garlic, jalapeño and cilantro in blender or food processor. Pulse until finely chopped, but not puréed. Add tomatoes, canned chilies, oil, lime juice, salt, cumin, vinegar, and tomato juice. Pulse until just chopped -- not too smooth. Correct seasonings, if necessary. Cover and refrigerate for about an hour before serving. Makes about 4 cups.

Texas 0302, a Soldiers' Angel in Texas

Fried Turkey

1 turkey, 14 lb max if frying
2 onions, quartered
1 bunch celery, rough chopped
8 medium carrots, rough chopped
1 c salt
1 c packed brown sugar
⅛ c Old Bay Seasoning
4 bay leaves
2 gal water
4 oranges, quartered
4 lemons, quartered
4 limes quartered

Heat water, onions, celery, carrots, salt, sugar, Old Bay, and bay leaves to a boil and reduce heat. Simmer for 30 minutes. Remove from heat and let cool. You are making a vegetable stock. While the stock is cooling, rinse the turkey well, making sure you REMOVE THE GIBLETS from the cavity. If the turkey has one of those pop-up indicators, remove it. Place the bird in a 5-gal container and add the stock and enough water to cover. Add the oranges, lemons, and limes, squeezing some of the juice into the stock. The bird will want to float. If too much is exposed, place a ceramic, not metal, plate on top with a clean, preferably unused, brick to hold the bird down. The brick can be sterilized in a 350 oven for 30 minutes. If you have room, place the container in the refrigerator. If you don't have room, place 5 lb ice, still in the bag, on top of the bird. This will eliminate the need for the brick. If it is cool outside, put the container on the back porch or in the garage. Secure the lid well so the critters can't get to the turkey. Let the bird brine for 12 to 24 hours. Prepare the fryer according to the manufacturer's directions. If using a propane-fired fryer, place it at least 20 feet from any structure you don't want to burn to the ground. NEVER use a propane fryer in the house or even the garage. I use an electric fryer with the heating element at the bottom of the oil, so no chance of fire. I prefer peanut oil because of the added flavor and health benefits. Make sure your guests are not allergic. Use enough oil to cover the turkey. That can be determined by placing the turkey in the fryer and covering with water. Mark the water line and empty the water and dry the fryer well. Never exceed the maximum fill line embossed on the fryer. (Read the directions!) When ready to fry, heat the oil to 400 to 425 F. The electric fryers have a thermostat to maintain temperature. Propane fryers will require adjustments. Remove the bird from the brine and rinse. Make sure none of the solids are in the cavity. Place the bird,

	breast side down in the fryer basket and CAREFULLY lower it in the oil. If using a propane fryer, I suggest 2 people use a broom stick to do this. Frying time is 3 min/lb + 5 min. For a 14-lb bird, that would be = 47 min. When done, CAREFULLY lift the basket out of the oil and let drain on cardboard. Part of the back may not brown, but that side goes down on the platter. Some of the skin may be stuck to the basket and the turkey's back bone may be very weak. Free the stuck skin and remove the turkey with tongs inserted in each end of the cavity. Silicone hot mitts work well, and an extra pair of hands would be helpful. I know, this sounds like a lot of work, but this will be the juiciest, best tasting turkey ever. If you don't want to fry, you can smoke the bird for 2 hours and finish in the oven, or you can skip the smoker and go straight to the oven. However you cook it, use a meat thermometer to make sure the internal temperature of the thigh is 180 F. I prefer brining to marinade injection because the flavor is more evenly distributed and the bird will be juicier. If you want to experiment, substitute Cajun crab boil or a spicy poultry rub for the Old Bay.

Mike Hendricks, a Soldiers' Angel in Irving, Texas

Green Bean Casserole

1 can French-style green beans, drained well 1 can white shoepeg corn, drained well 1 can cream of celery soup 2 bunches green onions, chopped ½ c grated Cheddar cheese ½ c sour cream 1 roll Ritz crackers, finely crushed ½ stick real butter, unsalted ½ - ¾ c grated Parmesan cheese	Mix green beans and corn in a small bowl, set aside. In a large bowl, mix soup, green onions, Cheddar cheese, and sour cream well. Add green beans and corn, mix well again. Pour into an 8 x 10 casserole dish and spread evenly. Melt butter in microwave, add Ritz crackers and mix well. Sprinkle evenly over the top of the green bean mixture. Sprinkle Parmesan cheese evenly over the top of Ritz crackers. Bake 40 minutes at 350 …ENJOY!!!!

Janet Stewart, a Soldiers' Angel in Dallas, Texas

Jalapeño Dressing

½ c coarsely chopped onion ¼ c sugar 2 T dry mustard 2 t salt 1 t coriander 1 c lemon juice or vinegar 3 c canola oil ¼ c minced jalapeño with some seeds 4 T chopped fresh cilantro	In food processor, blend first 6 ingredients for 1 minute. Continue to blend, and add oil in steady thin stream until emulsified. Turn off processor, and stir in jalapeño and cilantro with a spatula.

Texas 0302, a Soldiers' Angel in Texas

Jalapeño Cheese Square

1 lb Monterrey Jack cheese, shredded
1 lb Cheddar cheese, shredded
1 egg
1 c flour
1 can evaporated milk
1 jar sliced jalapeño, drained and chopped
    (small-to-medium jar; you may wish to
    add the juice, too, for extra spiciness)
	Place all ingredients in large mixing bowl, mix well. (Do not use electric mixer, mix with large mixing spoon.) Spread evenly in a 9 x 13 casserole dish and bake 50 minutes at 425. Cut into 1½-inch squares and serve WARM!

Janet Stewart, a Soldiers' Angel in Dallas, Texas

Mike's Jen-U-Wine Texas Chili

enough oil (vegetable, canola, or olive) to cover the bottom of a 4 qt stock pot
1 medium (baseball-size) onion, chopped
1 T minced garlic (3 cloves)
2 lb ground meat or 1 lb ground and 1 lb cubed (1/2 inch cubes)
½ c chili powder
1 T cumin
1 t oregano
1½ t cayenne
1½ t paprika
½ T salt
1 (6-oz) can tomato paste
1 (15-oz) can crushed tomato
1 (15-oz) can tomato sauce
1 (10-oz) can Rotel tomatoes
1 (12-oz) can V8
sugar (optional)
1 - 2 T dried cilantro (optional)

Note: beef (sirloin, round, or chuck) is good. Venison, veal, or pork are OK. Texas law forbids the use of turkey, chicken, or other weird things. Violation is punishable by exile to California. The addition of fillers such as beans, rice, or pasta is a hanging offense.

Heat the oil in the pot over medium heat and cook the onion until soft. Add the garlic and cook for another 2 minutes. Brown the meat with the onions and garlic. If using cubes, brown them first and then add the ground meat. While the meat is browning, mix the spices in a bowl. After the meat is browned, strain off the grease through a fine-mesh strainer to catch any stray meat. Return the strays to the pot and the pot to the heat. Add the spice mixture and stir to coat the meat. Add the tomato paste and mix to coat. Add the crushed tomatoes, tomato sauce, Rotel, and V8 and stir. Bring to a simmer and lower the heat. Simmer covered for 2 hours. After 1 hour check seasoning and adjust as desired with chili powder, cayenne and/or Tabasco. If desired, add sugar to counter act bitterness of tomatoes. Serve hot with crackers and grated cheese on the side.

Mike Hendricks, a Soldiers' Angel in Irving, Texas

Pork Roast with Mushroom Gravy

1 pork roast, 3 - 5 lb 1 c flour 1 T salt 1 t pepper 1 medium onion, chopped 2 cloves garlic, chopped 2 cans condensed cream of mushroom soup olive oil	Preheat oven to 350 degrees. Mix the flour, salt, and pepper in a bowl. (Note: you can substitute 1 envelope dry French onion soup mix for the salt.) Rub this mixture on all sides of the roast. Reserve any remaining mixture. Heat enough oil to cover the bottom of the skillet over medium heat. Sauté the onions for 2 minutes. Add the garlic and sauté for another 2 to 3 minutes. Don't burn the garlic. Using a slotted spoon, remove the onion and garlic to a paper towel to drain. If needed, add more oil to the skillet to cover the bottom. Brown the roast on all sides, using tongs to hold the roast on its ends. You should have a nice crust all over the roast. Place the roast in a Dutch oven. Pour the oil from the skillet over the roast, scraping the browned bits from the skillet. Add the mushroom soup, cover and place in the oven for 20 minutes. The soup will mix with the oil, flour, and pork drippings to make a gravy. After 20 minutes, check the thickness of the gravy and add water if needed. Continue to roast, checking the temperature of the roast every 5 minutes until a meat thermometer reads 165 F. Remove the roast to a platter and tent with foil to rest. The internal temperature should rise another 5 degrees F. If the gravy is too thick, add water. If it is too thin, add some of the reserved flour mixture over medium heat, stirring for a few minutes until the desired thickness is reached. Adjust the seasoning of the gravy as desired. Slice the roast and serve the gravy on the side.

Mike Hendricks, a Soldiers' Angel in Irving, Texas

Sausage Balls

3 c Bisquick 1 lb sausage (uncooked) ⅔ c milk 1 c grated Cheddar cheese	Mix all ingredients together. Roll into small balls. Put on ungreased cookie sheet. Bake at 350 for about 20 minutes. Drain on paper towels. Serve hot.

Martha Neyman, a Soldiers' Angel in Sherman, Texas

Smoked Brisket

1 beef brisket, what ever size you want

your favorite spice rub, enough to coat the brisket on all sides (You can buy it, concoct your own, or down load it from the Internet. I prefer those developed by Emeril Lagasse and Tyler Florence.)

12 oz beverage (Beer can work. Cola can work. I prefer Dr Pepper for its high sugar content.)

Serve with your favorite sides, slow-cooked beans, potato salad, slaw, etc. Suggested condiments: your favorite BBQ sauce (store-bought not recommended, but if you must!), sliced onion, pickles and, of course, peppers! A beverage may be needed to cool the mouth.

Rub the meat with the spices and wrap tightly with plastic. Refrigerate for at least 8 hours on a baking sheet. When ready to smoke, unwrap the meat and scrape off the excess rub. The good stuff has already permeated the meat. Prepare the smoker (if that's what you want to do). I use hardwood charcoal, usually oak. I avoid those little compressed briquettes. I get better heat. Supplement with wood chips for better smoke. (Mesquite or maple best compliment the beef). Smoke for at least 2 hours, keeping the temperature around 250 F. At this point you can elect to stay up all night, tending the fire and drinking beer or not. A bunch of us did that once. By the time the brisket was done, we were too tired and drunk to eat. What I do instead, remove the meat from the smoker to the rack on the broiling pan, fat side up. Pour the beverage into the bottom of the pan and tent tightly with foil. Place the pan in a 225 oven and go to bed. The idea is to let the meat cook very slowly while the beverage and drippings baste the meat. This can take 8 to 12 hours for a real brisket (12 to 15 lb), but you might want to cut back the time for a wimpy 5-lb slab. When you think it's done, stab the meat in the thickest portion with a meat thermometer. You're looking for 160 to 165 F. CAREFULLY remove the roasting pan from the oven (the bottom will be full with drippings) and let the whole thing rest, covered. Remove the meat to a cutting board and slice at an angle on the bias. You'll know the smoking was successful if you see a ¼ inch layer of brick red-smoke ring. Bon apatite, Ya'll!

Mike Hendricks, a Soldiers' Angel in Irving, Texas

Tex-Mex Cheesecake

Ingredients	Instructions
4 (8-oz) pkg 1/3 reduced fat cream cheese 1 pkg taco seasoning 2 small cans chopped green chilies 2 eggs 4 c grated Cheddar or Mexican Mix cheese 1 (8-oz) can nacho cheese dip or queso 1 (8-oz) container jalapeño dip chips, guacamole, sour cream, for serving chopped green onion, chopped tomatoes, black olives, cilantro, for garnish	Preheat oven to 300. Mix cream cheese, seasoning, chilies, eggs, and 2 cups cheese and pour in lightly greased spring form pan. Mixture will be thick. Bake for 1 hour (or in Colorado and other high altitudes 1 hour 15 minutes). Mix cheese dip, jalapeño dip, and remaining 2 cups cheese. Pour topping on cheesecake and bake another 15 minutes. Turn off the oven, open door, and let cool to room temperature. Loosen cake around edges with knife when cake is completely cooled. Cheesecake is best served at room temperature. Store in refrigerator.

Stephanie Brown, a Soldiers' Angel in Corsicana, Texas

Turkey Soup

Ingredients	Instructions

1 turkey carcass, not picked too cleanly
leftover turkey (white and dark meat), cut
    the turkey into bite-sized pieces
4 - 6 carrots, sliced
4 - 6 celery stalks, sliced
4 - 6 cloves garlic, chopped
1 medium bunch green onions, sliced
    (substitute 1-2 leeks if desired)
2 bay leaves
olive oil
2 - 4 c noodles or macaroni
2 c frozen green peas
chopped parsley (optional)
salt and pepper to taste
	Cover the bottom of the stock pot with oil and place on medium heat. Sauté the carrots, celery, green onions and garlic until just soft. Don't burn the garlic. Place the turkey carcass in the pot and cover with water. Add the bay leaves. Simmer for 15 minutes. Remove the carcass and add the noodles. Simmer for another 10 minutes. Add the turkey and peas and simmer another 5 minutes. Taste the broth for seasoning and adjust with salt and pepper. Remove the bay leaves and add the parsley. Remove from heat and let stand covered for 5 minutes. The flavor of the soup will depend on how the turkey was prepared. If it was brined with Cajun crab boil, it will be spicy. If a dry rub was used, that flavor will come through. If the bird was smoked, the soup will have a distinct smoky flavor. Turkey carcass can be split to fit into the pot.

Mike Hendricks, a Soldiers' Angel in Irving, Texas

Utah

Christmas Filled Cookies

1 c butter ½ c white sugar ½ c brown sugar 1 egg 3 T milk 1 t vanilla 3 c flour ½ t salt ½ t baking soda 2 c raisins or pitted dates ¼ t salt 1 c water or orange juice 2 T lemon juice	Cream butter and sugars until light. Add milk, egg, and vanilla. Sift dry ingredients together, stir into the wet, and pat into a ball. Chill 1 hour in a covered container. Meanwhile, make filling. In a blender, pulse 1 cup raisins/dates with ½ cup water/juice until finely ground. Pour into a saucepan. Grind remaining cup of fruit the same way, using more water/juice if necessary. Stir salt into ground fruit mixture in saucepan. Bring to a boil, then reduce heat to low and slowly simmer until liquid has evaporated, leaving a thick fruit mixture. Remove from heat and stir in lemon juice. Cool. Roll out chilled dough on lightly floured surface and cut into circles. Place about 2 teaspoons filling in the center of each circle, cover with a matching circle, and press edges together. Optional: using a small cookie cutter, cut a small heart or other design from the center of the top cookie, letting the filling show through. Bake at 375 for 10 to 12 minutes.

Karla Kelly, a Soldiers' Angel in St George, Utah

Easy Russian Pockets

canisters of ready-to-bake biscuits 1 small head of cabbage 1 small onion ½ clove garlic (or to taste) 1 t dill salt and pepper to taste	Dice the onion. Sauté with garlic in butter or oil until clear. Meanwhile, slice cabbage and boil until soft. Drain cabbage; add onion, garlic, and seasonings. When cool, spoon a tablespoon of the mixture into the center of a squished-down biscuit. Fold the edges of the biscuit in half and seal shut. Bake at 350 until golden brown. Note: There are a lot of variations you can make on these pirogi pockets: rice and hamburger, mashed potatoes and mushrooms, or, if you have a sweet tooth, maybe jam, sliced apples with cinnamon or strawberry and rhubarb. Experiment—these always taste good!

Mary Hedengren, a Soldiers' Angel in Provo, Utah

Funeral Potatoes

6 - 8 medium precooked potatoes (or a 2-lb pkg frozen hash browns) ¼ c diced onion 1 (10 ¾-oz) can cream of chicken soup (or cream of celery) ½ soup can milk 1 c sour cream salt and pepper to taste ¾ c corn flakes 3 T butter, melted 1 c sharp Cheddar cheese, grated	Funeral potatoes is an easy dish that you will find at a lot of funerals in Utah. Heat oven to 325. Thaw frozen potatoes or cook fresh potatoes and cut into cubes (skin on or peeled to taste). Place potatoes in a greased 2- to 3-quart casserole dish or a 9 x 13-inch cake pan. Sauté onion in 1 tablespoon butter and spread over potatoes. Combine soup, milk, sour cream, and salt and pepper to taste. For a creamier dish, add 2 to 3 tablespoons additional milk. Mix well. Spread sauce over potato/onion mixture. Melt butter and combine with corn flakes. Sprinkle corn flakes over mixture. Sprinkle cheese over mixture. Bake uncovered for 40 minutes or until hot and bubbly throughout. This recipe serves approximately 8, and is often served with ham and green beans.

Sfife, a Soldiers' Angel in Utah; Andrea Groen, a Soldiers' Angel in Bountiful, Utah

Honey Banana Bread

1¾ c all–purpose flour 1⅓ c mashed ripe banana ⅔ c packed brown sugar 4 T melted butter 2 T milk 2 T honey 1½ T cinnamon 1¼ t baking powder ½ t baking soda 2 eggs	Stir flour, baking powder, baking soda, and cinnamon. Set aside for later. In another bowl, mash bananas (about 2). Add eggs, melted butter, milk, and honey to bananas. Cream brown sugar into banana mixture. Slowly add dry mixture to bananas and sugar, stirring until moist after each addition. (Optional -- fold in nuts or dried fruit.) Turn batter into a lightly greased 8 x 4 x 2-inch bread loaf pan. Drizzle honey over top of loaf. Bake in a 350 oven for 60 to 65 minutes or until a wooden pick inserted near center comes out clean. Cool in pan for 10 minutes. Remove from pan; cool. For easiest slicing, wrap and store overnight. Makes one loaf. ENJOY!

Christine Macken, a Soldiers' Angel in Salt Lake City, Utah

Pasgetti Pizza

1 (16-oz) pkg spaghetti noodles ½ c milk ¾ t garlic powder 2 (15- or 16-oz) jars spaghetti sauce 1½ t oregano 3 c shredded Mozzarella cheese 1 (3½-oz) pkg sliced pepperoni 2 eggs 1 c (4 oz) shredded mozzarella ½ t salt	Break spaghetti noodles into 2-inch pieces. In large saucepan, cook according to package directions; drain and cool. Preheat oven to 400. In a large bowl, beat eggs lightly. Stir in milk, 1 cup Mozzarella cheese, garlic powder, and salt. Add cooked spaghetti noodles and stir until thoroughly combined. Grease a 10 ½ x 15½-inch jelly roll pan and spread the spaghetti noodles in pan. Bake for 15 minutes. Remove from oven and reduce temperature to 350. Spread spaghetti sauce evenly over spaghetti. Sprinkle with oregano, then 3 cups Mozzarella cheese. Top with pepperoni slices. Return to oven and bake 30 minutes longer. Let stand at room temperature for 5 minutes before cutting. Makes 10 (3 x 5 inch) pieces.

Andrea Groen, a Soldiers' Angel in Bountiful, Utah

Wedding Carrot Cake

3 c flour 2⅔ c white sugar 1 t salt 2 t baking soda 1 T cinnamon 1 c oil 3 eggs 2 c grated carrots 1 c coconut 1 t vanilla 1 c crushed pineapple, drained 1 c raisins (soak in hot pineapple juice for 15 minutes) 1 c chopped almonds 8 oz cream cheese, at room temperature 1 stick butter, cut into pieces, room temperature 1 c powdered sugar 1 t vanilla milk or cream	Cream sugar and oil until light; add eggs 1 at a time, beating to incorporate. Sift dry ingredients together and stir into the creamed mixture. Add carrots, coconut, drained pineapple, and plumped (drained) raisins. Add vanilla and nuts; mix well. Bake in 2 greased and floured round cake pans at 350 for 40 minutes. Cool in the pan, then turn out and frost. Use your favorite frosting to make it elegant, or cream cheese frosting to make it delicious. Place cream cheese in mixing bowl, beat slowly. When smooth, gradually add butter. Continue beating until smooth and combined. Gradually stir in sugar and vanilla. If it is too stiff, thin with a little milk or cream (very little) if desired.

Karla Kelly, a Soldiers' Angel in St George, Utah

Vermont

Maple Baked Beans

1 qt parboiled beans (red, kidney, etc) ⅛ t pepper ¼ t dry mustard 1 c maple syrup ¼ lb salt pork ¼ c chili sauce (optional) 1 small onion, diced 1 t salt 1 t ginger (optional)	Place 1/2 of the beans in a bean pot. Score salt pork and place on beans. Add remaining beans. Mix 1/2 cup maple syrup and the other ingredients and pour over the beans. Fill the pot with boiling water. Cover and bake in slow oven (300) for 4 hours. Remove cover, add remaining syrup and bake for 1/2 to 1 hour. It may be necessary to add water during baking.

Kathy Martell, a Soldiers' Angel in Vermont

Virginia

Cornbread Salad

1 pkg Hidden Valley ranch dressing
1 c milk
1 c sour cream
1 c mayonnaise
1 (15-oz) can corn
2 (16-oz) cans pinto beans, drained and
    lightly rinsed
½ c fresh green pepper, chopped
3 fresh tomatoes, diced
½ c green onions/or regular onions,
    chopped
2 c shredded Cheddar cheese
	Mix dressing in a bowl with milk, sour cream, and mayonnaise. Sit this mixture in the fridge for about 30 minutes. While this is chilling, bake a pan of cornbread. Take cornbread and crumble up with your fingers into a 9 x 13 pan. Layer corn, beans, and green peppers on top of the cornbread. Pour dressing over top. Add tomatoes, onions, and cheese. Cover and refrigerate for about an hour. You can top with crispy crumbled bacon if you like.

Nothinbutgrass, a Soldiers' Angel from Virginia

Gut Busters

hot dog buns hot dogs chili (homemade or canned) Fritos shredded Cheddar cheese	Heat up the chili and pour it over a plate of Fritos. I normally put some butter on the buns and fry them over the stove, but you could also put them in the toaster. When they are toasted, tear them up in little pieces and put them on the plate over the chili. Cut up the cooked hot dog and put it on the plate as well. Smother with cheese and enjoy! If you like the cheese to be melted on top, zap it in the microwave for about 5 to 10 seconds. I hope you enjoy this VERY American family recipe. My grandmother use to make these for my Uncle's baseball games. He played minor league in Missouri. They were a huge hit at the food stand, and have become a New Years tradition in my family.

Whitney Salahub, a Soldiers' Angel in Fairfax, Virginia

Hattie Terry's Stewed Tomatoes

1 can tomatoes Ritz crackers sugar to taste salt to taste pepper to taste butter	Place tomatoes in a saucepan to heat. Add sugar, salt, and pepper and enough crackers to thicken. Nanny would only use Ritz crackers. This is my grandmother's recipe.

Sharon Moody, a Soldiers' Angel in Mechanicsville, Virginia

Jackie Cooper's Crab Meat Yummies

1 c crab meat 1 jar Old English sharp cheese ½ t garlic salt ½ t seasoned salt 1 stick butter 2 T Miracle Whip salad dressing 6 English muffins, split in half	Mix cheese, salts, butter, and salad dressing. Add crab meat and mix gently. Spread mixture on muffin halves. Freeze. Cut in quarters while frozen. These can be kept frozen in freezer bag for several weeks. Broil as needed, about 4 to 5 minutes or until bubbly. Watch carefully. The Crab Meat Yummies are delicious and go very fast at a party. Make more than you think you will need. This is my cousin's recipe.

Sharon Moody, a Soldiers' Angel in Mechanicsville, Virginia

Margie Kelley's Batter Bread

1c corn meal 3 t baking powder 2 t salt 2 eggs 2 c boiling water 2 c sweet milk 1 T lard, melted in baking dish	Pour 2 cups boiling water over corn meal. Beat in salt, baking powder, and well-beaten eggs. Add milk. Pour into well-greased pan or dish in which lard was melted. Bake at 450 until brown and a knife put into the center comes out clean. This is my mother's recipe.

Sharon Moody, a Soldiers' Angel in Mechanicsville, Virginia

Lucille Walden's Sweet Potato Pie

4 medium sweet potatoes 4 eggs 1 c sugar ¼ c melted butter 1 t lemon extract 1 large can evaporated milk nutmeg or cinnamon 2 9-inch pie shells	Cook sweet potatoes and mash. Melt butter and mix with sugar. Add remaining ingredients. Pour into unbaked 9-inch pie shells and bake at 350 about 45 minutes. This recipe makes 2 pies. This is my aunt's recipe.

Sharon Moody, a Soldiers' Angel in Mechanicsville, Virginia

Emma Stone's Mashed Turnips	
1 large turnip per person salt and pepper to taste 1 T sugar ham hock or butter	This is my great-grandmother's recipe. Wash, peel, and quarter turnips. Place in pan and cover with water. Add salt and boil until soft. After turnips are cooked, drain off water. Add pepper, salt, and sugar, then mash. Turnips can be cooked with ham hock or add butter when ready to mash.

Sharon Moody, a Soldiers' Angel in Mechanicsville, Virginia

Washington

Apple Sorbet

4 Golden Delicious apples, pared, cored, and sliced ½ c sugar ¼ c water 1½ t lemon juice ¼ t ground cinnamon	Combine apples, sugar, and water in saucepan; cover tightly and simmer 10 to 15 minutes or until apples are tender. Cool. Puree in food processor or blender until smooth. Stir in lemon juice and cinnamon. Pour into freezer-proof 8-inch square pan; cover, and freeze 1 to 2 hours or until almost firm. Spoon into large electric mixer bowl; beat with chilled beaters until mixture is light and foamy. Return to pan; freeze until firm.

Dina Katkansky, a Soldiers' Angel in Battle Ground, Washington

Clam Chowder

½ c butter 1½ large onions, chopped ¾ c flour 1 qt shucked clams, with liquid 6 (8-oz) jars clam juice 1 lb boiling potatoes peeled and chopped 3 c half-and-half salt and pepper to taste ½ t chopped fresh dill	Melt butter in large pot over medium heat. Add onions and sauté until clear. Stir in flour and cook over low heat stirring frequently for 2 to 4 minutes. Set aside to cool. In a separate pot, bring clams and clam juice to a boil. Reduce heat and simmer for 15 minutes. In a small saucepan, cover peeled potatoes with water. Bring to a boil and cook until potatoes are tender, about 15 minutes. Drain and set aside. Slowly pour hot clam stock into butter/flour mixture while stirring constantly. Continue stirring and slowly bring to a boil. Reduce heat and add cooked potatoes. Mix in half-and-half, salt and pepper and chopped dill. Heat through but do not boil.

Jo Gregory, a Soldiers' Angel in Olympia, Washington

Dungeness Crab Cakes

1 lb Dungeness crab meat 1 egg, beaten 2 t yellow mustard ½ c mayonnaise ¼ t Worcestershire sauce ½ c diced onion ½ t ground black pepper ¾ t crab seasoning 1 c fresh grated bread crumbs	Put crabmeat in mixing bowl and add beaten egg. Mix lightly. Add remaining ingredients in order listed. Form mixture into desired size. Fry in skillet with vegetable oil on medium to high heat (about ½ inch oil in skillet). Fry on one side until golden brown and turn over on other side to get the same.

Jo Gregory, a Soldiers' Angel in Olympia, Washington

Hot Cocoa Brownies

1 c flour 1 c hot cocoa mix 1 c sugar 1 t baking powder ½ c chocolate chips 2 eggs ¾ stick butter 1 t vanilla	Mix eggs, butter, and vanilla. Add dry ingredients and stir. Batter will seem too dry, but just mix thoroughly. Spread in 8 x 8 inch pan and bake at 350 for 30 minutes.

Rebekah Fox, a Soldiers' Angel in Snohomish, Washington

Knock You Naked Brownies

1 box German chocolate cake mix 1 c chopped nuts ⅓ plus ½ c evaporated milk ½ c melted butter 60 vanilla caramels, unwrapped (14 oz) 1 c semisweet chocolate chips	In a large mixing bowl, combine dry cake mix, nuts, 1/3 cup evaporated milk, and melted butter. Press half of the batter into the bottom of a greased 13 x 9 x 2 glass baking dish. Bake at 350 for 8 minutes. In the microwave or top of a double boiler, melt caramels with remaining 1/2 cup evaporated milk. When caramel mixture is well mixed, pour over baked layer. Cover with chocolate chips. Chill for about an hour until the caramel is hard. Press the remaining batter on top of morsels. Return to oven and bake 28 minutes (or less for gooier brownies). Cool before cutting.

Jo Gregory, a Soldiers' Angel in Olympia, Washington

Nordy Bars

½ c butter 12 oz butterscotch chips ½ c firmly packed brown sugar 2 eggs 1½ c flour 2 t baking powder ½ t salt 2 t vanilla 12 oz chocolate chips 2 c miniature marshmallows 1 c chopped pecans	In a saucepan, melt butter over medium heat. Add butterscotch chips and brown sugar, stirring until melted. Remove from heat. Stir in eggs. Add flour, baking powder, and salt. Mix well. Stir in vanilla. Cool completely. It must cool completely, no cutting corners in order for it to turn out right! When cooled, stir in chocolate chips, marshmallows, and pecans. Spread into greased 9 x 13 inch pan. Bake at 350 for 25 minutes. Remove from oven and cool completely. Again, cool completely! Cut into squares and serve. Cut into 24 or 36 bars.

Amy Doggett, a Soldiers' Angel in Gig Harbor, Washington

Simple Salmon Bake	
2 lb salmon fillet 6 large carrots 6 celery stalks seasoned salt	In a food processor, chop carrots and celery finely (small chunks). Sprinkle seasoned salt on salmon fillet and cover with chopped carrots and celery. Bake in oven at 350 for 30 to 45 minutes depending upon how well done you like your salmon. This recipe is very versatile in that you may chop most any vegetable instead of or in addition to the carrots and celery.

Teri Scott, a Soldiers' Angel in Port Angeles, Washington

West Virginia

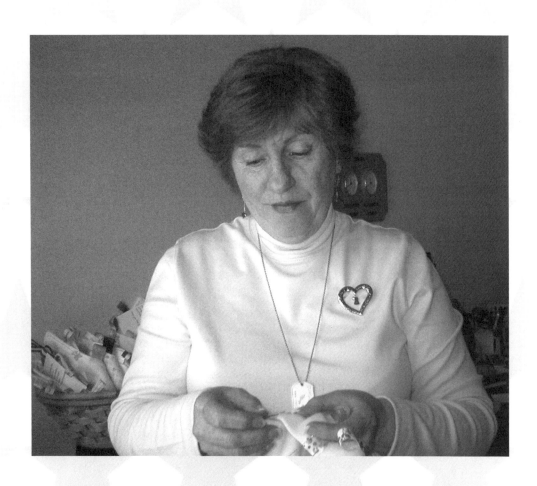

West Virginia Hillbilly Chili

2 lb ground beef 2 large cans tomato juice 1 medium onion, diced 1 pkg Taco seasoning mix 2 large cans pinto or kidney beans, drained 2 t hot sauce	Put all contents into a large crock pot and let cook on low for 8 hours.

Judi Brinegar, a Soldiers' Angel in North Carolina

Lazarus Restaurant Bread Pudding with Whiskey Sauce

¾ lb bread, French or sourdough ¼ c pecans, toasted 12 oz butter, melted, divided 2 c white sugar 1 t salt 10 eggs, large 5½ c milk 1 t vanilla 2 c powdered sugar, sifted 1 oz whiskey	Break bread into medium pieces. Add pecans and 4 oz melted butter. Arrange in 9 x 13 inch pan. Blend 8 eggs, salt, and white sugar lightly with wire whip. Add vanilla and milk. Blend and strain. Pour over bread and nuts in pan. Bake at 350 in pan of water for 20 to 25 minutes. Test with knife. For whiskey sauce, melt 8 oz butter. Whip in sifted powdered sugar. Fold in 2 beaten eggs. Add whiskey. Serve warm over the pudding.

Janet Mattson, a Soldiers' Angel in West Virginia

Mountaineer Cheese Ball

8 oz sharp cheese 8 oz spreadable cream cheese 1 t finely chopped onion 1 t finely chopped green pepper 1 T Worcestershire sauce ½ t lemon juice 1 c finely chopped pecans crackers and breadsticks, for serving	Mix everything but pecans in a bowl; dump cheese mix onto pecan-covered wax paper. Pull wax paper sides up around mixture to form ball, pressing pecans into sides of cheese mix. Cover bottom of small bowl with pecans and dump cheese mix into bowl, cover tightly and refrigerate until slightly stiff. May serve from bowl or dump onto plate; use various crackers or breadsticks for dipping. This cheese ball is very easy to spread.

Kim Vorholt, a Soldiers' Angel in West Virginia

Taco Dip

1 lb ground chuck ½ c chopped onion 1 pkg Taco seasoning 1 can of cheese dip sour cream, chopped tomatoes, shredded lettuce, shredded cheese, jalapeños to taste, taco chips	Brown beef and onions and drain the fat. Add seasoning and cheese dip. Stir and heat for 20 minutes on low to medium heat. Ladle large spoonful of meat mixture onto plate, Spread sour cream over mixture, layer with tomatoes, lettuce, cheese, and jalapeños. Set out taco chips to dip.

Kim Vorholt, a Soldiers' Angel in West Virginia

Wisconsin

Beer and Cheese Pretzel Dip

3 (8-oz) bricks of plain cream cheese 1 pkg Hidden Valley Ranch powdered dressing mix (Not dip mix) ½ -1 c beer 1 – 2 c shredded Cheddar cheese pretzels, for serving	Allow cream cheese to sit out for at least a half hour to soften. Mix cream cheese, powdered dressing mix, and beer until well blended. Stir in desired amount of shredded Cheddar cheese. Can be served right away, but is better if refrigerated for a few hours first. Serve with any kind of pretzel.

Jessica Stoller, a Soldiers' Angel in Sheboygan, Wisconsin

Brats/Beer

brat links 1 (12-oz) bottle beer condiments, for serving	Open the bottle of beer and pour most, okay, 3/4 of it into a large cooking kettle, drink the last 1/4 of the bottle (á la Julia Child and wine). Add water so that when brats are added, the water covers them. Bring to a boil and then turn off the kettle. Start the barbeque. Drain off the liquid and when barbeque is ready cook them sausages until done. Serve immediately with whatever condiments your family likes and whatever side dishes are the favorites. Enjoy!

Kathy McTavish, a Soldiers' Angel in Chippewa Falls, Wisconsin

Bratfest

bratwurst 2 cans beer 1 onion	To make really good bratwursts, mix beer and onion. Add the bratwurst. Bring contents to simmer. NEVER boil brats. This bursts the casing. Throw out the beer/onion mixture. Put the brats on a covered grill. Grill for 10 to 15 minutes and turn. YUM!

Iris Wilde, a Soldiers' Angel in Wisconsin

Cheesy Chili

2 lb ground beef 2 medium onions, chopped 2 garlic cloves, minced 3 (10-oz) cans diced tomatoes and green chilies, undrained 1 (28-oz) can diced tomatoes, undrained 2 (4-oz) cans chopped green chilies ½ t pepper 2 lb Velveeta cheese	In a large saucepan, cook the beef, onions, and garlic until meat is no longer pink; drain. Stir in tomatoes, chilies, and pepper; bring to a boil. Reduce heat, simmer, uncovered, for 10 to 15 minutes. Stir in cheese until melted. Serve immediately or allow to cool before freezing. May be frozen for up to 3 months.

Lara Brzezinski, a Soldiers' Angel in De Pere, Wisconsin

Chicken Alfredo and Rice Casserole

1 (10-oz) pkg Alfredo pasta sauce ½ c milk 2½ c cooked white or wild rice 2 c cubed cooked chicken 1 c frozen peas ⅓ c sweet red peppers ¼ c slivered almonds ½ t dried basil 1 c soft bread crumbs 1 T butter, melted	Preheat oven to 350. In large bowl. combine pasta sauce and milk. Stir in rice, chicken, peas, sweet peppers, nuts, and basil. Transfer to 1 ½-quart casserole dish. Bake, covered, 30 minutes. Uncover and stir. Combine bread crumbs and melted butter; sprinkle on top. Bake, uncovered, 20 to 25 minutes. Let stand 5 minutes.

Lara Brzezinski, a Soldiers' Angel in De Pere, Wisconsin

German Potato Salad

4 large potatoes 5 thick slices of bacon, diced 1 c chopped onions ¼ c wine vinegar ¼ c water ¼ c sugar salt and pepper to taste	Boil potatoes in their jackets, then peeled and sliced. Fry bacon. Mix potatoes, bacon, and onion. Mix remaining ingredients as a dressing and pour over potatoes.

Iris Wilde, a Soldiers' Angel in Wisconsin

Make-ahead Spinach Manicotti

1 (15-oz) carton ricotta cheese
1 (10-oz) pkg frozen chopped spinach
  (thawed and squeezed dry)
1½ c (6 oz) shredded mozzarella cheese,
  divided
¾ c shredded Parmesan cheese, divided
1 egg
2 t minced fresh parsley
½ t onion powder
½ t pepper
⅛ t garlic powder
2 (28-oz) jars spaghetti sauce w/meat
1½ c water
1 (8-oz) pkg manicotti shells

In a large bowl, combine ricotta, spinach, 1 cup mozzarella, 1/4 cup Parmesan, egg, parsley, onion powder, pepper, and garlic powder. Combine the spaghetti sauce and water: spread 1 cup sauce in an ungreased 13x9x2in baking dish. Stuff uncooked manicotti with spinach mixture; arrange over sauce. Pour remaining sauce over manicotti. Sprinkle with remaining mozzarella and Parmesan. Cover and refrigerate overnight. Remove from the refrigerator 30 minutes before baking. Bake, uncovered at 350 for 40 to 50 minutes or until heated through This recipe is one that my grandma used to make and it has been modified a little so it can be a great do-ahead dish!

Janet Hohn, a Soldiers' Angel in Blanchardville, Wisconsin

Wyoming

Pork and Butternut Squash Stew

2 lbs lean pork loin chops, cubed (bite-size) 4 - 5 potatoes, peeled, cubed (bite-size) 4 - 5 carrots, peeled, diced 2 parsnips, peeled, diced 1 butternut squash, peeled, cubed (bite-size) 1 large sweet onion, diced 4 - 6 c chicken broth 1 T Parisian Bonnes Herbes * 1 t dried French thyme 1 t salt fresh ground pepper to taste 3 T butter or margarine, softened (use 4 T if using 6 c broth) 3 T flour (use 4 T if using 6 c broth) * Parisian Bonnes Herbes is a combination of chives, dill weed, basil, French tarragon, chervil, and white pepper that is sold by Penzey's Spices. You can substitute another blend of spices that you might prefer.	Preheat oven to 350. Place pork, potatoes, carrots, parsnips, squash, and onion in a large (8 qt is best) roasting pan. Pour in enough chicken broth to just cover pork and vegetables; stir in seasonings. Cover roasting pan and bake 2 hours; then remove from oven (but do not turn oven off). In a small bowl, blend softened butter (or margarine) with the flour using a spatula. Stir the mixture into the hot stew until thoroughly blended. Place roasting pan back into the oven and cook another 35 to 40 minutes until sauce is thickened.

Heather Lynne Harmon, a Soldiers' Angel in Matthews, North Carolina

Sheepherder Chili

3 lb ground beef 4 T dried onions ¼ c chili powder 1 T cumin 2 T Worcestershire sauce 1 t garlic powder ¼ t cayenne pepper salt and pepper 1 t dried oregano 1 t vinegar 1 can stewed tomatoes 1 can tomato sauce	Brown the meat in a heavy pot, drain off the fat, and add all the other ingredients. Simmer for at least 2 hours, adding water as needed. Thicken with flour if desired (preferably masa harina or ground-up corn tortillas).

Donna Allon (fefifauxfumgirl), a Soldiers' Angel in Alabama